# The Gospel According to David Foster Wallace

## NEW DIRECTIONS IN RELIGION AND LITERATURE

This series aims to showcase new work at the forefront of religion and literature through short studies written by leading and rising scholars in the field. Books will pursue a variety of theoretical approaches as they engage with writing from different religious and literary traditions. Collectively, the series will offer a timely critical intervention to the interdisciplinary crossover between religion and literature, speaking to wider contemporary interests and mapping out new directions for the field in the early twenty-first century.

## ALSO AVAILABLE FROM BLOOMSBURY:

*Blake. Wordsworth. Religion*, Jonathan Roberts
*Dante and the Sense of Transgression*, William Franke
*Do the Gods Wear Capes?*, Ben Saunders
*England's Secular Scripture*, Jo Carruthers
*Forgiveness in Victorian Literature*, Richard Hughes Gibson
*Glyph and the Gramophone*, Luke Ferretter
*The Gospel According to the Novelist*, Magdalena Mączyńska
*Jewish Feeling*, Richa Dwor
*John Cage and Buddhist Ecopoetics*, Peter Jaeger
*Late Walter Benjamin*, John Schad
*The New Atheist Novel*, Arthur Bradley and Andrew Tate
*Rewriting the Old Testament in Anglo-Saxon Verse*, Samantha Zacher
*Victorian Parables*, Susan E. Colón
*The Willing Suspension of Disbelief*, Michael Tomko

## FORTHCOMING:

*Faithful Reading*, Mark Knight and Emma Mason
*Romantic Enchantment*, Gavin Hopps
*Sufism in Western Literature, Art and Thought*, Ziad Elmarsafy

# The Gospel According to David Foster Wallace

Boredom and addiction in an age of distraction

**ADAM S. MILLER**

Bloomsbury Academic
An imprint of Bloomsbury Publishing Plc

B L O O M S B U R Y
LONDON • OXFORD • NEW YORK • NEW DELHI • SYDNEY

**Bloomsbury Academic**
An imprint of Bloomsbury Publishing Plc

50 Bedford Square
London
WC1B 3DP
UK

1385 Broadway
New York
NY 10018
USA

www.bloomsbury.com

**BLOOMSBURY and the Diana logo are trademarks of Bloomsbury Publishing Plc**

First published 2016

© Adam S. Miller, 2016

Adam S. Miller has asserted his right under the Copyright, Designs and Patents Act, 1988, to be identified as Author of this work.

All rights reserved. No part of this publication may be reproduced or transmitted in any form or by any means, electronic or mechanical, including photocopying, recording, or any information storage or retrieval system, without prior permission in writing from the publishers.

No responsibility for loss caused to any individual or organization acting on or refraining from action as a result of the material in this publication can be accepted by Bloomsbury or the author.

**British Library Cataloguing-in-Publication Data**
A catalogue record for this book is available from the British Library.

ISBN:  HB: 978-1-4742-3698-0
       PB: 978-1-4742-3697-3
     ePDF: 978-1-4742-3700-0
     ePub: 978-1-4742-3699-7

**Library of Congress Cataloging-in-Publication Data**
A catalog record for this book is available from the Library of Congress.

Series: New Directions in Religion and Literature

Typeset by Integra Software Services Pvt. Ltd.

*For Jamie Smith*

# Contents

Abbreviations ix
Preface x
Acknowledgments xiv

1   Books 1
2   Heads 5
3   Maps 9
4   Taxes 13
5   Contortions 15
6   Addiction 17
7   Desire 21
8   Despair 25
9   Distraction 29
10  Watching 31
11  Assassins 35
12  Irony 39
13  Masks 43
14  Beauty 47
15  Time 51
16  Deskwork 55
17  Sewage 59
18  Size 63
19  Silence 65
20  Immersion 69

| | | |
|---|---|---|
| **21** | Indifference | 73 |
| **22** | Boredom | 77 |
| **23** | Awareness | 81 |
| **24** | Heroes | 83 |
| **25** | Revelations | 87 |
| **26** | Abiding | 91 |
| **27** | Bodies | 95 |
| **28** | Prayer | 99 |
| **29** | Clichés | 103 |
| **30** | Epiphany | 107 |

Afterword 109

Permissions 115

Bibliography 117

Index 119

# Abbreviations

**CD**    Burn, Stephen J., ed. *Conversations with David Foster Wallace*. Jackson: University Press of Mississippi, 2012.

**NU**    Dostoevsky, Fyodor. *Notes from Underground*. Translated and edited by Michael R. Katz. New York: W. W. Norton and Company, 2001.

**AS**    Dreyfus, Hubert and Sean Dorrance Kelly. *All Things Shining: Reading the Western Classics to Find Meaning in a Secular Age*. New York: Free Press, 2011.

**FA**    Franzen, Jonathan. *Farther Away*. New York: Farrar, Straus and Giroux, 2013.

**RT**    Lipsky, David. *Although of Course You End Up Becoming Yourself: A Road Trip with David Foster Wallace*. New York: Broadway Books, 2010.

**BF**    Wallace, David Foster. *Both Flesh and Not: Essays*. New York: Little, Brown and Company, 2012.

**CL**    Wallace, David Foster. *Consider the Lobster and Other Essays*. New York: Little, Brown and Company, 2005.

**IJ**    Wallace, David Foster. *Infinite Jest*. New York: Little, Brown and Company, 1996.

**PK**    Wallace, David Foster. *The Pale King*. New York: Little, Brown and Company, 2011.

**SF**    Wallace, David Foster. *A Supposedly Fun Thing I'll Never Do Again: Essays and Arguments*. New York: Little, Brown and Company, 1997.

**TW**    Wallace, David Foster. *This Is Water: Some Thoughts, Delivered on a Significant Occasion, about Living a Compassionate Life*. New York: Little, Brown and Company, 2009.

# Preface

I'm serious about television. I watch it religiously. When I watch, I watch with forty years of practiced intensity. I turn off the lights and sit on the floor and cross my legs. I scoot up close to the warm plasma screen. I prefer to watch alone. Even if I run out of time to pray or mow the lawn or read to my kids, I find time to watch TV. I watch almost every day, usually at the same set times, and I'm careful about what I watch. I read up on what's streaming now and what's coming next. I curate a list. I'm looking for a particular kind of thing. I'm loose with genres but I'm looking, across the board, for something that is smart and beautiful and tinged with tragedy. Drama or comedy or documentary or March Madness, it needs to skirt the absurd without succumbing to absurdity. It needs a literary mood. It needs to hint at absent gods. It needs mythos.

I'm careful about this because I want to wring more from TV than just distraction. I want transcendence. David Foster Wallace recognizes the impulse. "Television offers way more than distraction. In lots of ways, television purveys and enables *dreams*, and most of these dreams involve some sort of transcendence of average daily life" (SF 39). When I watch TV, I'm looking for something that, a hundred years ago, I would have looked for at a Mass or in a mosque or deep inside a Zen monastery. I'm looking for what used to be, more or less exclusively, the business of religion. I want to worship. And clearly, regardless of my real religious commitments, at least part of me thinks my best shot at immediate transcendence is through a piece of furniture in my living room. Otherwise, why all the care and devotion? The thing's significance is framed, centered, and enshrined on my wall: mounted glass and electric light, a consumer-friendly transcendence machine—religion in a box. These days, churches aren't competing with other churches for true believers, they're competing with the National Football League.

This project is bound to fail. I know this both in principle and practice. Disappointment is inevitable. I'm aiming at an idol that, however clever and beautiful, can't bear the weight of my devotion. While the impulse to worship, the impulse to aim myself at something, is primal, the failure of our idols is just as certain. Their failure is as original as our wanting them to succeed. TV is no different. It's no better or truer a god. I know this. But it hasn't stopped me from queuing up again.

What's to be done? Even if you disavow religion (or television) altogether, you can't avoid worship. The impulse to worship is a human problem, not a religious problem. "In the day to day trenches of adult life," Wallace reminds us, "there is actually no such thing as atheism. There is no such thing as not worshipping. Everybody worships" (TW 98–101). Try as you might, there's no place to hide from your yen for transcendence. And, more, there's no place to hide from the consequences of its failure. Choose your gods wisely but pretty much anything you worship "will eat you alive" (TW 102). Getting eaten alive by your idols is part of what it means to be human.

It's tempting to read this moment of disappointment, this moment when worship fails and transcendence collapses back into distraction, as cause for either condemnation or vindication. As grounds for condemnation, the moment of disappointment can be taken as more good evidence that the religious project is pointless. Worship doesn't work. It never has before and now, despite whatever local heights you may have reached, it has definitely failed again. But the opposite verdict is also possible. This disappointment can be read as a vindication of religion, as good evidence that worshiping anything other than the one true God will cannibalize you every time. You weren't wrong to worship, you just aimed at the wrong thing. Pick the right thing next time. The failure of a false god vindicates your hunger for the true one.

This polemic can go either way but, in the end, both readings seem thin. They both think worship is about finding an object that won't disappoint. And, as polemic, they both miss something vital about the character of this disappointment, about the curvature of the arc that worship describes. Cribbing from David Foster Wallace, this book argues for a third reading. This third way doesn't see the moment of disappointment as a failure of religion *or* as a failure to be religious. Rather, it reads the moment of disappointment as pivotal to the character of worship. It reads this failure of transcendence as a feature (not a bug) of religion itself. In fact, it holds that one main goal of religion is to induce this disappointment.

This third reading offers a contemporary version of a very old religious idea. This old idea has the shape of a paradox: to save God you must lose God. This idea claims that there is a moment of inversion at the heart of worship, a twist in the loop of transcendence that renders it, Möbius-like, continuous with immanence. This twist joins both sides—transcendence and immanence—as a single surface. If, with dogged persistence, you rise along the line of transcendence you will reach a point of inversion in your ascent that will, without ceremony or explanation, return you to immanence. This homecoming will hurt a bit. It will feel like failure. It will disappoint.

If you worship (and you do), this moment will come. You'll pass the point of inversion, the spell of transcendence will break, and, with that break, you'll lose your religion. You'll give up. You'll have a mid-life crisis. You'll get divorced. You'll wonder what it all means. You'll stop buying new clothes or going to church or wanting to impress people or reading the Bible or believing in the magic of television. You'll be sad. This sadness is risky. It's risky because it threatens to obscure the urgent revelation shining at the heart of your loss: the revelation that the end of worship was, all along, immanence and that, though your head may invent a thousand ways of escaping this world, the point of religion is to return you to it.

There are two elements at play in worship: the aiming and the aimed at. The aiming itself is hungry but unstable. The aimed at is nameable but evasive. Invested by your aiming with the hope of satisfaction, with the hope of escape and transcendence, the aimed at becomes an idol. This is what defines an idol. An idol is an object invested by your attention with the hope of transcendence. An idol is an object turned mirror. It's an object of worship that reflects the hopeful intensity of the aiming you've pointed at it.

But, again, your idol can't meet this expectation. No idol can. The hope that it could is a mirage. And when that idol fails—when it disappoints your aiming and shows itself without transcendence: immanent, disheveled, disenchanted—there will be a moment, perhaps quite brief, when all that remains of worship is a pang of raw aiming. This moment when it looks like your worship has failed is the religious moment. This is the revelation. This moment allows the aiming itself to appear. And it is in the aiming *itself*, not in the object aimed at, that God is most clearly manifest. This is the epiphany. Disappointed by the idols you've fashioned in your head's own image, bored by their familiarity, floundering free of any object, the nature and weakness of worship can blink into view. What it means to be human can blink into view. Attention itself can come to your attention. And, more, attention can come to your attention as what gives (to you) both yourself and the world. In your disappointment, the aiming that's common to every idol can show itself as "the subsurface unity of all things" and then, in this light, the world will no longer appear as something that might satisfy but, instead, as something "sacred, on fire with the same force that lit the stars" (TW 93).

The religious moment is not the moment when—whoosh!—the magic happens and the world seems full of a pantheon of idols able to satisfy. It's the moment when—fshzzzt—the spell breaks, the credits roll, the lights come back up, and the world must be cared for, again, as just whatever it is. Come back to where you are, Wallace urges us. Pay attention. "One day at a time. Easy does it. First things first. Courage is fear that has said its prayers. Ask for help. Thy will not mine be done. It works if you work it. Grow or go. Keep coming back" (IJ 270). Whatever you do, keep coming back.

# Acknowledgments

My thanks to Jenny Webb and Blair Hodges.

# 1

# Books

David Foster Wallace hung himself in 2008. He was forty-six years old. He published three collections of short stories, three collections of essays, and two novels. At the time of his death, he was working on a third. His second novel, *Infinite Jest*, may be the best thing written in a generation.

I'm aware, as Jonathan Franzen warns, of the temptation to treat Wallace as some brand of postmodern saint, wrecked and hallowed by his mental illness. I recognize that "the people who knew David least well are most likely to speak of him in saintly terms" (FA 39). Perhaps inevitably, a compensatory impulse to hagiography followed his suicide. This effect, Franzen suggests, may even have been part of what Wallace blackly intended.

> But if you happened to know that his actual character was more complex and dubious than he was getting credit for, and if you also knew that he was more lovable—funnier, sillier, needier, more poignantly at war with his demons, more lost, more childishly transparent in his lies and inconsistencies—than the benignant and morally clairvoyant artist/saint that had been made of him, it was still hard not to feel wounded by the part of him that had chosen the adulation of strangers over the love of the people closest to him. (FA 38–39)

Franzen may be right about this, but I can't speak to it. The "Saint David" meme doesn't interest me. I'm drawn to these books—and, especially, to what they have to say in a religious vein—because, with

Wallace, I think life's basic questions have little to do with sainthood and, instead, everything to do with what it means to be "a fucking human being."

On Wallace's account, this is the point of fiction. This is the point of a thousand-page novel. "Fiction's about what it is to be a fucking *human being*. If you operate, which most of us do, from the premise that there are things about the contemporary U.S. that make it distinctively hard to be a real human being, then maybe half of fiction's job is to dramatize what makes it tough. The other half is to dramatize the fact that we still *are* human beings, now. Or can be" (CD 26). This is a strong brief for fiction writing. And if there is something like a "gospel" according to David Foster Wallace, I think it teeters on this line between the *fact* of our already being human and the possibility that, despite everything, we still *could* be.

The altar boy in me wants to clean up Wallace's language, but I think we need to let it stand. Though bracing, "fucking" condenses much of what Wallace wants to say about the human condition. It names both the tragicomic vulgarity that colors our living and how that vulgarity is tangled up with our hunger for intimacy. Fiction matters, Wallace thinks, because it can facilitate this intimacy. It can help us be human by making us less lonely. By dramatizing the boredom and addiction that make it hard to be human in our age of distraction, it can show us that we're not alone in our heads. It can show us that we're not alone in feeling what we feel. Even if what we feel is lonely.

The more you tend to get stuck in your own head, the more you'll resonate with Wallace's work. Granted, this isn't the same for everyone. For some people, consciousness seems mostly benign. But for others, consciousness can coil inward in a way that makes the head metastasize. As Dostoevsky's underground man says: "I remain firmly convinced that not only is being overly conscious a disease, but so is being conscious at all" (NU 6). For most of us that diagnosis is too strong, but its worry channels Wallace's own.

Wallace's fiction treats this disease by way of vaccination. His writing reproduces the streaming chatter in our heads and, by sharing it, repurposes it as an inoculation against the loneliness it otherwise tends to feed. This is Wallace's great talent: he can mimic, with disturbing and hilarious precision, the many voices in our heads. As David Lipsky put it, Wallace's work is so arresting because it had done a thing that was casual and gigantic; he'd captured everybody's brain voice. The talk show with its solo guest; the yammer while you're commuting the office halls, kissing, musing in the bathroom. All the different thought categories—books, *Jurassic Park*, weird business terms of art, curses, how things could suddenly make you depressed or happy for no reason at all—it was the way you flattered yourself your brain really might sound, if you'd just devote the time to shelving and organization. (RT xxviii–xxix)

Reading Wallace and finding the stammering voices of our brains on his pages, we feel less alone. We're reminded that our skulls are open on one side. We're reminded that it's possible to face outward and pay attention. And we're reminded that, however we might strain after transcendence, we are already here and already human.

Wallace's work dramatizes how a feedback loop of ingrown thoughts can stifle our living. And in playfully dramatizing it he lampoons, to our relief, our gullibility in falling again and again for the same manic lures. This, he shows us in set piece after set piece, is what it means to be human and this is what's happening in our heads.

# 2

# Heads

The plot of *Infinite Jest* wanders through a host of characters and storylines, but its rambling dependably returns to the problem abridged in its opening line: "I am seated in an office, surrounded by heads and bodies" (IJ 3). This is the book's whole schema. Packed into a single sentence, it has only two terms: heads and bodies. *Infinite Jest* is one long spiraling meditation on how heads and bodies can either come together or fall apart.

In the book's first scene (a scene that, chronologically, comes last), heads and bodies have emphatically fallen apart. Hal Incandenza is auditioning for a tennis scholarship at a major university. Hal is a solid player but not professional material. His ankle, while functional, is torn up. But Hal has other advantages. Like his engineer father and grammarian mother, he's whip-smart. He describes himself as the kind of kid who might jump in a taxi and yell: *to the library, and step on it!* But, meeting with university administrators, he faces skepticism about the excellence of his academic work. His recent test scores have plummeted. Something fishy is going on. His entourage keeps fielding questions and offering assurances, but the administrators won't have it. They want to hear from Hal himself. They badger away until, when Hal finally opens his mouth to speak, we discover that he can't. He can croak but he can't speak. Sounds that he thinks are words are, to everyone else in the room, just horrifying noise.

At some point, something happened to Hal and words are now lost to him. We never learn for certain what happened—drugs? terrorists? slime?—but, whatever it was, Hal is now trapped inside his own head. He tries to tell the administrators he's still "in" there, but he can't make himself understood. His head has come loose from the heads and bodies that surround him. Hal has suffered the fate of Toni Ware's doll in *The Pale King*:

> After Houston her favorite doll had been the mere head of a doll, its hair prolixly done and the head's hole threaded to meet a neck's own thread; she had been eight when the body was lost and it lay now forever supine and unknowing in weeds while its head lived on. (PK 55)

Hal is an unthreaded doll's head, his body lost in the weeds. Trapped in his own brain, he can no longer make himself heard.

Hal's problem is extreme but not unusual. Heads float free from bodies all the time, especially when they lack the focus that connects them. Heads come loose when we get distracted. They come loose when we lose the ability to pay attention. Given the critical importance of such focus, it should be no surprise that for most us, Wallace says, "the whole ballgame [is] perspective, filtering, the choice of perception's objects" (PK 15). Filtered connection is the key. Focused attention is what threads a head back onto a body.

Without this ability to pay attention, everything gets hazy and we end up glued to the couch, dazed and disembodied, remote control in hand, flipping through TV channels without actually watching anything. We end up like Wallace's weed-smoker who, while waiting for another delivery of pot, gets so anxious that he couldn't even "distract himself with the [TV] because he was unable to stay with any one entertainment cartridge for more than a few seconds. The moment he recognized what exactly was on one cartridge he had a strong anxious feeling that there was something more entertaining on another cartridge and that he was potentially missing it" (IJ 26). Anxious and restless, he can't zero in. He can't bring his head to bear. If, in Wallace's work, there is something like a doctrine of "original sin"—something like a common condition that simultaneously defines and compromises our being human—it's this. We're distracted. We're sinners because we can't put down the remote. We can't stop changing channels.

# HEADS

This confluence of distraction and desperation is dangerous because the two wind each other up. The more anxious and desperate we feel, the more distracted we become. And the more distracted and disconnected we become, the more anxious and desperate we feel. The faster they spin, the dizzier we get. When distraction and despair "explode into a hall of mirrors," we get funhouses for heads (PK 188). Hour by hour, day by day, our anxiety accumulates a reflective quality that does little more than amplify itself.

In the thick of a workday, you may be busy enough to ignore how much of an echo chamber the head tends to be. But when you're forced to sit still for a moment, the cacophony is hard to ignore. When a person sits in silence in a traffic jam, the "yammering mind-monkey of their own personality's dark, self-destructive side" can promptly take center stage (PK 316). Or, when you lie down at night in a dark bed, exhausted and praying for sleep, the head's tractionless spinning can assert itself. The body wants to sleep but the head just spins. "Self-consciousness, the chattering head, the cackling voices, the chocking-issue, fear versus whatever isn't fear, self-image, doubts, reluctances, little tight-lipped cold-footed men inside your mind, cackling about fear and doubt, chinks in the mental armor" (IJ 118). We lie down to rest and then promptly replay the most stressful parts of the day. We worry about the mortgage. We fantasize about the bodies of people we don't love. We wonder how long our health can possibly last, how long our employment can possibly hold, and how long our children can possibly bear with us. The general mood is eschatological. We parade the world's end before our closed eyes.

But even sleep, when your head has short-circuited, is no magic cure. If you manage to sleep, you'll still have to dream and, what's more, your head will still be waiting for you in the morning. Even if you get as far as sleep's forgetting, you may still end up like Hal Incandenza. For Hal, his trouble with his head gets so bad that

> it wasn't just nightmares and saliva. It was as if his head perched on the bedpost all night now and in the terribly early A.M. when Hal's eyes snapped open immediately said Glad You're UP I've Been Wanting To TALK To You and then didn't let up all day, having at him like a well-revved chain-saw all day until he could finally try

to fall unconscious, crawling into the rack wretched to await more bad dreams. 24/7's of feeling wretched and bereft. (IJ 796)

With heads like this, even sleeping feels like work. Your head gets louder, your days get longer, and you feel tired all the time. You end up, like Jesus, with no place to lay your head.

# 3

# Maps

By design, *Infinite Jest* doesn't conclude so much as expire. Given their trajectories, its converging plot lines look like they would have crossed and crescendoed a few hundred pages past the book's end. One of these plot lines follows Hal Incandenza, his family, and his fellow tennis prodigies at the elite Enfield Tennis Academy in Boston. A second line follows Don Gately and the residents of the Ennet Drug and Alcohol Recovery House. Gately is a recovering addict and live-in staffer. The halfway house sits just down the hill from the tennis academy. The third line follows a group of wheelchair-bound French-Canadian terrorists bent on acquiring the master copy of a film (titled "Infinite Jest") that is, reportedly, lethally entertaining. The film is said to be so enthralling that one look at it will ruin your head. The film was made by Hal's father and may be buried in a pile of discount video cartridges at the halfway house. The terrorists hope to acquire the master copy, broadcast it nationwide, and lobotomize, in one stroke, the whole of an US audience unable to resist watching, even at the cost of their own lives, the promise of something so spectacularly entertaining.

Two violent melees punctuate Wallace's patient interweaving of these three narrative lines. The first comes about a third of the way through and involves students from the Enfield Tennis Academy. The second falls about two-thirds of the way through and involves residents from the halfway house. The second battle is, I think, more important for the plot. But the first is more important thematically.

In *Infinite Jest*'s skewed vision of the near future, the United States has strong-armed Canada and Mexico into joining the

Organization of North American Nations (O.N.A.N.) and a day is set aside for celebrating the union. The eighth of November is designated as "Interdependence Day." Every year, dozens of kids from the tennis academy get together and spend the holiday playing a massively complex war game called Eschaton that splices geo-politically realistic role-playing, wildly arcane mathematical models of nuclear warfare, and the phenomenally accurate lobbing of tennis balls by semi-professional twelve-year-olds in lieu of actual warheads. The game takes all day and sprawls over four contiguous tennis courts that jointly function as a rough map of the planet.

This time, the game goes south when a bare-knuckle fight breaks out over the difference between the game's map of the world and the world that map is meant to represent. Thematically, this section is critical because one of Wallace's favorite synonyms for head is "map." Head is map and body is world. Things fall apart when we can't properly connect the map between our ears with the world at our feet.

On this brisk November morning, the trouble starts when a fuzzy yellow warhead is launched at Karachi and a distracted Otis P. Lord, Eschaton's reigning master of ceremonies, fails to personally witness whether the hit was direct or indirect. An argument starts and Lord's distraction plants a seed of anxiety about the map's integrity. "It's an uneasy moment: a dispute such as this would never occur in the real God's real world, since the truth would be manifest in the actual size of the actual wienie roast in the actual Karachi. But God here is played by Otis P. Lord" and Lord is only human (IJ 333).

The problem is compounded when fat flakes of snow start to fall and one player, emboldened by the confusion, "all of a sudden gets the idea to start claiming that now that it's snowing the snow totally affects blast area and fire area and pulse-intensity and maybe also has fallout implications, and he says Lord has to now completely redo everybody's damage parameters before anybody can form realistic strategies from here on out" (IJ 333). This is "an obvious instance of map-not-territory equivocationary bullshit," but it's exactly the kind of equivocationary bullshit that people are, in general, prone to fall for (IJ 337).

Michael Pemulis, emeritus master of ceremonies, jumps to Lord's defense. "'It's snowing on the goddamn *map*, not the *territory*, you dick!' Pemulis yells" (IJ 333). But it's too late. The lines are blurred and chaos ensues. Instead of calmly and intermittently lobbing warheads at designated targets, kids start pegging each other with blazingly wicked forehands and claiming that, as a result, they've just vaporized their opponents. Pemulis's whole face turns red with anger. Through clenched teeth he explains that

> players themselves can't be valid targets. Players aren't inside the goddamn game. Players are part of the *apparatus* of the game. They're part of the map. It's snowing on the players but not on the territory. They're part of the *map*, not the cluster-fucking *territory*. You can only launch against the *territory*. Not against the *map*. It's like the one ground-rule boundary that keeps Eschaton from degenerating into chaos. Eschaton gentlemen is about logic and axiom and mathematical probity and discipline and verity and *order*. You do not get points for hitting anybody real. Only the gear that *maps* what's real. Pemulis keeps looking back over his shoulder to the pavilion and screaming "*Jay*sus!" (IJ 338)

No one is listening. Balls are rocketing around the court as players empty their arsenals, rackets get tossed aside as kids go after each other with their bare hands, and in the midst of the commotion a raging giant of an adolescent girl plows straight into the wheeled cart that houses the hardware used to run the game's simulations. "There's a noise like the historical sum of all cafeteria accidents everywhere. 3.6-MB diskettes take flight like mad bats across what uncovered would be the baseline of Court 12" and the system's "monitor and modem and Yushityu chassis, with most of Eschaton's nervous system on its hard drive, assume a parabolic southwest vector" (IJ 342). The system crashes to the ground, "the Yushityu's hard-drive chassis makes an indescribable sound as it hits the earth and its brightly circuited guts come out," and "the color monitor lands on its back with its screen blinking ERROR at the white sky" (IJ 342).

This is the problem. Maps get taken for territories and ERROR results. You lose track of what's body and what's just head. And the more time you spend stuck in your head, ignoring the world, hungry for transcendence and distraction, the more superficial your life becomes. And the more superficial your life becomes, the more undead you feel. After a while, "everything becomes an outline of the thing. Objects become schemata. The world becomes a map of the world" (IJ 693). After a while, everything becomes an idol, a mirror, an empty suit, a map that outlines nothing but the path you've plotted to escape from a world full of bodies.

# 4

# Taxes

The trouble with worlds and bodies is that, unlike maps, they're taxing. They're big, complicated, unwieldy, chaotic. Bodies have inscrutable agendas all their own. Maps reduce this disorder to a more navigable outline. But that reduction is hard work and, in the end, what distinguishes a map from the world is the world's ongoing resistance. This resistance is a crucial feature of what's real.

In *The Pale King*, Wallace's unfinished novel, the US tax code epitomizes the cost and resistance proper to the world of real bodies. The tax code, like a body, is a mystery hidden in plain view. It's the kind of thing that is both too ordinary and too complex for the head to understand. And, as *The Pale King*'s fictional David Wallace notes, "to these qualities ... I would respectfully add one more: boredom. Opacity. User-unfriendliness" (PK 82). The real is boring and user-unfriendly. It resists attention, it's "a fact-pattern the bulk of which was entropic and random" (PK 16). The real is full of noise and, more, it's full of patterns that look like noise.

If you choose to keep your head in the world, you'll have to value this noise. You'll have to value the world's insistence on disappointing your attempts at worship. You'll have to pay attention and swallow your pride and side with the noise and opacity and user-unfriendliness of the real. You'll have to side with what's taxing. You may even have to go to work for the Internal Revenue Service and learn how to read 1040B's. When interviewed for a "Your IRS Today" documentary, one anonymous tax examiner (video file #973876118) urges you to just go ahead and side with the inevitable:

> Check out the blowing wind, man. Join up with the side that *always* gets paid. We shit you not. The side of the law and the force of the law, the side of the tide and gravity and that one law where everything always gradually gets a little hotter until the sun up and blows. Because you got your two unavoidables in life, just like they say. Unavoidability—now that's power, man. Either be a mortician or join the Service, if you want to line yourself up with the real power. Have the wind at your back. (PK 105)

There is some fatalism here. But there is also a realism tempered by an appreciation for the "unavoidables." Life's unavoidables tend to be technical, opaque, and user-unfriendly. As a result, an accountant/father figure tells us, there are "only two kinds of people in the world—namely, people who actually understood the technical realities of how the real world worked … and people who didn't" (PK 235). This division is a little too neat, but there's still something to it. There are people who are connecting with the world of bodies and there are those who aren't. One key to doing the former is to confess the inadequacy of your maps. You have to confess "that no matter how smart you thought you were, you are actually way less smart than that" (IJ 201). You have to confess that your head is way smaller than the world and that the world's ways are clearly not your ways.

# 5

# Contortions

One of *The Pale King*'s most striking fragments is about a boy contortionist. The boy has asthma and needs to stay inside. It's raining on the day that, bored, the boy starts bending himself into new shapes and his life's work accidentally begins. In the months and years that follow, the boy patiently works away at twisting his joints and loosening his body's grip on itself. He works mainly in his bedroom and he keeps the door closed. The carpet is white shag. There's a tree outside the window. Sometimes his father sits outside the boy's door and listens, trying to tell what's going on inside. The father is worried and doesn't know what to do. The boy's mother is gone. The boy, though, takes his work seriously.

> Every whole person has ambitions, objectives, initiatives, goals. This one particular boy's goal was to be able to press his lips to every square inch of his own body. His arms to the shoulders and most of the legs beneath the knee were child's play. After these areas of his body, however, the difficulty increased with the abruptness of a coastal shelf. The boy came to understand that unimaginable challenges lay ahead of him. He was six. (PK 394)

Kiss by kiss, the boy's goal is to swallow himself.

The work is hard but the boy finds some help. A sympathetic chiropractor tutors him in how to stretch and twist his body into new shapes. Practicing with great discipline, he manages increasingly powerful contortions that unlock access to more and more of his body. The work itself is sufficiently compelling that it is never "established precisely why this boy devoted himself to the goal of being able to press his lips to every square inch of his own body. It is not clear even that he conceived of the goal as an 'achievement' in any conventional sense. Unlike his father, he did not read Ripley and had never heard of the McWhirters—certainly it was no kind of stunt. Nor any sort of self-eviction; this is verified" (PK 400). The work has a logic of its own that the boy need not understand to pursue. The laser-like intensity of his self-love almost burns through its own vanity.

But the work, no matter how pure, is destined to fail. It ignores basic facts about the body and the world. Only the boy's willful naiveté about the nature of his body gives the project hope. "Insights or conceptions of his own physical 'inaccessibility' to himself (as we are all of us self-inaccessible and can, for example, touch parts of one another in ways that we could not even dream of with our own bodies) or his complete determination, apparently, to pierce that veil of inaccessibility—to be, in some childish way, self-contained and -sufficient—these were beyond his conscious awareness. He was, after all, just a little boy" (PK 401). Bodies are defined in part by their "self-inaccessibility." One of the things that makes a body your own is that, unlike someone else's body, you can't touch all of it. Bringing this inaccessibility to an end would effectively put an end to that body's being yours. In order to be, in some childish way, self-contained, the head would have to absorb the body or leave that body behind. Either version of the dream is a disaster that amounts to the same thing: a disembodied head.

The irony at work in the boy's ambition is important to see. He is driven by his head's inaccessible desire to make all of his body accessible to his head. But the truth runs counter to this: the body isn't part of the head, the head is itself part of the body. The boy senses this absurdity, but he's come too far to acknowledge it. "He did not yet know how, but he believed, as he approached pubescence, that his head would be his. He would find a way to access all of himself. He possessed nothing that anyone would ever call doubt, inside" (PK 407).

This, in stark terms, is what the head's self-promoting fantasy looks like: frictionless self-access, flawless transparency, a body that no longer has enough substance to get in its own way, lips capable of kissing themselves. This idolatry takes a thousand forms.

# 6

# Addiction

Addiction is one of Wallace's most persistent themes. He sees the basic shape of it everywhere. Drugs, TV, movies, tennis, sex, house cleaning, grammar, you name it: everything is fair game for loops of idolatrous compulsion. Nothing is out of bounds. Anything can become an idol invested by your worship with a promise it cannot keep. Addiction is, for Wallace, a general name for all manner of head-imploding diseases. When people suffer from this compulsion, "they identify their whole selves with their head, and the Disease makes its command headquarters in the head" (IJ 272).

Reflecting on the occupants of *Infinite Jest*'s halfway house, Wallace notes how chemical addictions often come intertwined with a second sort of addiction. As part of a running five-page list of observations about addiction (each of which begins abruptly with "That ... "), he notes: "That most Substance-addicted people are also addicted to thinking, meaning they have a compulsive and unhealthy relationship with their own thinking" (IJ 203). The compulsion to abuse a substance gets twisted up with an addict's compulsion to worry and distraction: each addiction feeds the other.

If, though, one of the two has some priority, Wallace takes it to be our addiction to thinking. When heads come unthreaded from bodies, when worlds are traded for maps, everything starts to feel insubstantial. And when life starts to feel insubstantial, you may be tempted to abuse substances. Wallace hints at this connection between feeling insubstantial and the abuse of substances by consistently writing "Substance abuse" with a capital "S." He does so because part of what's at stake in substance abuse is a hunger for some uppercase Substance that could, for once, satisfy desire and appease the head's hunger for transcendence.

But this hunger for some final Substance is a dead end. You can't get rid of it. To the extent that you try, the hunger's persistence will worry a groove in your brain and the groove will wear deeper and deeper until your mind gets stuck. "The cute Boston AA term for addictive-type thinking is: *Analysis-Paralysis*" because the head's circular thinking makes real action in the world increasingly difficult (IJ 203). Paralysis results. You freeze up at the mirages generated by your worrying. And then the only thing you can do is repeat the idolatry that didn't work before. Notice, Wallace says,

> that 99% of compulsive thinkers' thinking is about themselves; that 99% of this self-directed thinking consists of imagining and then getting ready for things that are going to happen to them; and then, weirdly, that if they stop to think about it, that 100% of the things they spend 99% of their time and energy imagining and trying to prepare for all the contingencies and consequences of are *never good*. Then that this connects interestingly with the early-sobriety urge to pray for the literal loss of one's mind. In short, that 99% of the head's thinking activity consists of trying to scare the everliving shit out of itself. (IJ 203–204)

The fears generated by all this self-directed thinking are compounding. These fears—self-confirming and, frequently, self-fulfilling—swamp your head. They scare the life out of you. And then, scared lifeless and shitless, your impulse will be to pray with your whole mind for God to relieve you of that mind.

Wallace gives us a smaller-scale version of this same problem in *The Pale King*. There, a perspiration-prone David Cusk also discovers the dangers that attend this kind of recursive thinking. "It was in public high school that this boy learned the terrible power of attention and what you pay attention to. He learned it in a way whose very ridiculousness was part of what made it so terrible. And terrible it was. At age sixteen and a half, he started to have attacks of shattering public sweats" (PK 91). The trouble for Cusk is that, once the attacks start, the primary trigger quickly becomes his own fear of having such an attack. He's always been a sweaty kid, but now his head is involved and he becomes self-conscious about his sweatiness. He spends all his time worrying about what he might look like, "his face gleaming with a mixture of sebum and sweat, his shirt sodden at the collar and pits, his hair separated into wet little creepy spikes from his head's running sweat" (PK 92). And then, almost inevitably, he can only imagine his classmates making the harshest of judgments. The whole business is self-perpetuating. "The fear of it could bring it on. He did not truly begin to suffer until he understood this fact, an understanding he came to slowly at first and then all of an awful sudden" (PK 93). Once the snake starts eating its own tail, Cusk is in serious trouble.

More, it doesn't take long for these mental processes to calcify into something quasi-institutional and take on a bureaucratic life of their own. As *The Pale King*'s knee-weakeningly gorgeous Meredith Rand says of her time in a mental hospital: "Once things became institutionalized then it all became this artificial, like, organism and started trying to survive and serve its own needs just like a person, only it wasn't a person, it was the opposite of a person, because there was nothing inside it except the will to survive and grow as an institution" (PK 488). Cusk's own head risks becoming a non-person, a corporate home for circular fears and desires that do little more than feed their own will to self-perpetuation. When this happens, Cusk himself is bound to disappear and become just a "creature of the system," a ghost in the institutional machine of his now autonomous head (PK 546).

# 7

# Desire

Lyle lives in the Enfield Tennis Academy weight room. He is the academy's resident guru. He's old. He sits lotus style on the weight room's towel dispenser, dressed in Spandex, and he doesn't move from that spot. He lives off the sweat of students. Once they've worked up a good sheen on the weights or in the sauna, Lyle takes questions from students and offers oracular advice in return—if they first let Lyle lick the sweat off their foreheads. Often, the line to see Lyle is long. "Sometimes Lyle will listen and shrug and smile and say 'The world is very old' or some such general Remark and decline to say much else. But it's the way he listens, somehow, that keeps the saunas full" (IJ 387).

LaMont Chu comes to see Lyle on Interdependence Day. It's already dark outside. When his turn comes, Chu, "high-gloss in a white towel and wristwatch, haltingly confesses to an increasingly crippling obsession with tennis fame" (IJ 388). The obsession has taken up residence. He desperately wants to be Michael Chang. "He wants to get to the Show so bad it feels like it's eating him alive. To have his pictures in shiny magazines, to be a wunderkind, to have guys in blue I/SPN blazers describe his every on-court move and mood in hushed broadcast clichés. To have little patches with products' names sewn onto his clothes. To be soft-profiled" (IJ 388). Chu is eleven years old. He's talented, but his performance is starting to suffer. Sometimes, lately, the "cold clenched fear of losing has itself made him lose" (IJ 388). His head is full of projections and his fixation on these projected futures is displacing the present. "The obsession with future-tense fame makes all else pale" (IJ 388). His brain is curling up into a tight little ball.

Lyle understands. He's seen this before. Getting eaten alive by your idols is routine. "LaMont," Lyle begins, "the world is very old. You have been snared by something untrue. You are deluded. But this is good news. You have been snared by the delusion that envy has a reciprocal. You assume that there is a flip-side to your painful envy of Michael Chang: namely Michael Chang's enjoyable feeling of being-envied-by-LaMont-Chu. No such animal" (IJ 389). This, too, is characteristic of desire. Desire naturally assumes that its own intensity is strong evidence for the existence of a correspondingly intense satisfaction. Desire assumes some correlative Substance. It invests its idol with the promise of release. But there is no such animal. "You burn with hunger for food that does not exist" (IJ 389). Envy has no reciprocal. Desire wants to desire. It blindly wants, more than anything else, its own perpetuation. Nothing will satisfy it. "Fame is not the exit from any cage," Lyle tells LaMont (IJ 389). "After the first photograph has been in a magazine, the famous men do not *enjoy* their photographs in magazines so much as they fear that their photographs will cease to appear in magazines" (IJ 389). Desire is adaptive. No matter how great the success, its intensity is easily and upwardly adjustable. Success is no Substance. In itself, it's just raw material for new fears and desires. Chu, though, is like the rest of us who "still worship the carrot," who "still subscribe to the delusive idea that the continent's second-ranked fourteen-year-old feels exactly twice as worthwhile as the continent's #4" (IJ 693).

Wallace returns to this topic on multiple occasions. Take, for instance, Hal Incandenza's grandfather who frets, like Chu, about being successful. He's an aspiring actor with designs on Hollywood. For a few years he rides some smalltime success in TV spots selling garbage bags, but then work peters out. Failing, he breaks down and confesses his fears to his son, James Incandenza.

> It's my fault, Jim, home so much, limping around, ruined knees, overweight, under the Influence, burping, nonslim, sweat-soaked in that broiler of a trailer, burping, farting, frustrated, miserable, knocking lamps over, overshooting my reach. Afraid to give my last talent the one shot it demanded. Talent is its own expectation, Jim: you either live up to it or it waves a hankie, receding forever.

Use it or lose it, he'd say over the newspaper. I'm ... I'm just afraid of having a tombstone that says HERE LIES A PROMISING OLD MAN. It's ... potential may be worse than none, Jim. Than no talent to fritter in the first place, lying around guzzling because I haven't the balls to ... God I'm I'm so *sorry*, Jim. You don't deserve to see me like this. I'm so scared, Jim. I'm so scared of dying without ever being really *seen*. Can you understand? (IJ 168, ellipses original)

But the grandfather's case is not especially instructive because it leaves the fantasy intact. He is tormented, like Chu, by the thought of a success he doesn't have, by a promise and potential that's unrealized. The trouble is that, as a result, Hal's grandfather never discovers that fame and achievement, even if he'd had them, wouldn't have brought that torment to an end.

Hal's own father, on the other hand, turns out to be a phenomenal and polymathic success. Hal had "a father who lived up to his own promise and then found thing after thing to meet and surpass the expectations of his promise in" (IJ 173). But it still didn't work. Success was no panacea. Hal's father "didn't seem just a whole hell of a lot happier or tighter wrapped than his own failed father" (IJ 173). Being successful or "having a lot of money does not immunize people from suffering or fear" (IJ 204). Suffering can expand to fill whatever space is available. Eventually the suffering is too much for Hal's father and, one day, little Hal comes home to find that his father has committed suicide and that he's done it—with all the flair of his trademark technical ingenuity—by figuring out how to cook his own head in a microwave.

The Enfield Tennis Academy hires professional counselors to help students prepare themselves for the trauma of success. The counselors are critical because "unprepared-goal-attainment-trauma is unbelievably gruesome and sad" (IJ 437). Achievement can be more dangerous than failure. At least failure leaves you with the fantasy of some uppercase Substance. But imagine what happens when "you attain the goal and realize the shocking realization that attaining the goal does not complete or redeem you, does not make everything for your life '*OK*' as you are, in the culture, educated to assume" (IJ 680). When this happens, you're left to "face this fact that what you had thought would have the meaning does not have the meaning when you get it" (IJ 680).

Most of us never get this far. We may have our suspicions, but the pull of desire is too strong. How, we wonder, could a desire this intense lack a correlative satisfaction? We worry the edges of our idolatry with the fear that we won't get what we want, but we rarely have the guts to worry that getting it wouldn't fix the trouble in our heads anyway. Imagine that "you become just what you have given your life to be. Not merely very good but the best" (IJ 680). Then what? "You are doomed if you do not have also within you some ability to transcend the goal" (IJ 680).

# 8

# Despair

The impulse to worship is relentless and if no Substance can be found to quell your desire, then desperation may compel you to cut it off at the root. In the opening paragraph of a long nonfiction piece about pornography, Wallace wincingly reports that

> the American Academy of Emergency Medicine confirms it: Each year, between one and two dozen adult US males are admitted to ERs after having castrated themselves. With kitchen tools, usually, sometimes wire cutters. In answer to the obvious question, surviving patients most often report that their sexual urges had become a source of intolerable conflict and anxiety. The desire for perfect release and the real-world impossibility of perfect, whenever-you-want-it release had together produced a tension they could no longer stand. (CL 3)

Measures like these follow from exhaustion. They follow from the kind of exhaustion that comes from believing without reservation in the possibility of a "perfect release" and then, time after time, never finding it.

Though, here again, success may be worse than the exhaustion of failure. Be careful what you wish for because achieving perfect release would be functionally equivalent to death. It would release you not only from desire but also from life itself. The desire to be done with desire by way of total satisfaction is, ironically, the "appetite to choose death by pleasure if it is available to choose" (IJ 319). At first blush, such a choice seems extreme. But the likelihood of our choosing death by pleasure, wherever possible, is what makes the French-Canadian terrorists' threat of a fatally entertaining film like "Infinite Jest" a real danger. If they managed to broadcast it, we might well watch it. A fatal peek might be irresistible.

The human drive to completion is intense and fundamental. "We are all dying to give our lives away to something, maybe. God or Satan, politics or grammar, topology or philately—the object seemed incidental to this will to give oneself away, utterly. To games or needles, to some other person. Something pathetic about it. A flight-from in the form of a plunging-into" (IJ 900). This is the sleight of hand to watch for. A "flight-from" that takes the form of a "plunging-into," a going all-in on desire that's actually a hope of freedom from its grip. A hunger for an uppercase Substance capable of extinguishing desire looks, on the face of it, like a commitment to desire. These are the false gods we worship: whatever coincidental Substances might promise perfect release. God has himself regularly been conceived along these lines. And the heavens where he resides have often been described as a finally satisfying place reachable only by way of death. "The original sense of *addiction*," Hal tells us, "involved being bound over, dedicated, either legally or spiritually. To devote ones' life, plunge in" (IJ 900).

The promise of a finally perfect release is big business and, in this regard, Wallace's dissection of what we want from a luxury Caribbean cruise is telling. *Harper's Magazine* occasioned the essay by sending Wallace on a one-week luxury cruise and asking him to record, quasi-journalistically, whatever Wallace-esque observations he cared to share. It doesn't take him long to settle on a theme. The essay immediately zeroes in on what Wallace takes to be the real product a luxury cruise means to sell.

> All of the Megalines offer the same basic product. This product is not a service or set of services. It's not even so much a good time (though it quickly becomes clear that one of the big jobs of the Cruise Director and his staff is to keep reassuring everybody that everybody's having a good time). It's more like a feeling. But it's also still a bona fide product—it's supposed to be *produced* in you, this feeling: a blend of relaxation and stimulation, stressless indulgence and frantic tourism, that special mix of servility and

condescension that's marketed under configurations of the verb "to pamper." This verb positively studs the Megaline's various brochures. (SF 260)

A ticket on a luxury cruise is supposed to buy a perfect blend of relaxation and stimulation, of "flight-from" disguised as "plunging-into." This professionally managed path to perfect release is neatly summarized by the word "pamper." "The fact that contemporary adult Americans also tend to associate the word 'pamper' with a certain *other* consumer product is not an accident, I don't think, and the connotation is not lost on the mass-market Megalines and their advertisers" (SF 261).

How many commercials have you seen where toddlers, beautifully lit against a baby blue backdrop, trundle around cloud nine in their perfectly fitted Pampers? These babies are in heaven, pampered and carefree. They've laid down the burden of their desire at the feet of adults who know what they're doing and can manage a perfect release for them. They can shit wherever and whenever they'd like. They don't need to do anything.

> How long has it been since you did Absolutely Nothing? I know exactly how long it's been for me. I know how long it's been since I had every need met choicelessly from someplace outside me, without my having to ask or even acknowledge that I needed. And that time I was floating, too, and the fluid was salty, and warm but not too-, and if I was conscious at all I'm sure I felt dreadless, and was having a really good time, and would have sent postcards to everyone wishing they were here. (SF 268)

Pampering like this is a retreat from life by way of the womb. But this womb is a fantasy and to end up back there would amount to a disavowal of life. It would amount to a kind of ante-life where our baby heads float peacefully in saline while our troublesome adult bodies are set aside.

> The promise is not that you can experience great pleasure, but that you *will*. That they'll make certain of it. That they'll micromanage every iota of every pleasure-option so that not even the dreadful

corrosive action of your adult consciousness and agency and dread can fuck up your fun. Your troublesome capacities for choice, error, regret, dissatisfaction, and despair will be removed from the equation. (SF 267)

The trouble, Wallace finds, is that the promise to pamper the despair right out of you does itself induce despair. Because the promise is a fraud. It won't work. It can't. The cruise will happily sell you a ticket to some uppercase Substance, but it can't deliver. If you save up your money and make it to the cruise, you'll find only the same thing LaMont Chu would have found on the far side of envy: exhaustion tinged with that special brand of despair that comes not from being denied what you want but from getting it.

# 9

# Distraction

When he concentrates, Shane Drinion levitates. Usually the distance between his butt and his seat is too small to be visible. But if his concentration deepens, he may float a few inches into the air. Drinion is good at concentrating, especially when the material is difficult, and this makes him very good at examining tax returns. Occasionally, when he is entirely focused on what he's doing, he may even go a bit higher. "One night someone comes into the office and sees Drinion floating upside down over his desk with his eyes glued to a complex return, Drinion himself unaware of the levitating thing by definition, since it is only when his attention is completely on something else that the levitation happens" (PK 485). It's a neat trick, but Drinion doesn't care.

One night after work, Drinion goes to a bar with some co-workers. He drinks a little and nods along with the conversation. Mostly he's quiet. As the evening draws on, the group diffuses and, eventually, he ends up alone with the alluring Meredith Rand. Rand's not sure what to make of Drinion, but she warms to the fact that Drinion can pay attention to what she's saying without her charms making him defensive or distracted. As she talks, Drinion just looks her in the eye, intently but matter-of-factly. So Rand opens up and, soon, starts telling him about the time she spent in a psychiatric ward. While there, Rand says, she realized something that is both painfully true and utterly ordinary. She realized that it's possible to leave a "childhood freedom and completeness behind but still remain totally immature. Immature in the sense of waiting or wanting some magical daddy or rescuer to see you and really know and understand you and care as much about you as a child's parents do, and save you. Save you from yourself"

(PK 498). This immaturity takes different forms "but really it's all the same, which is wanting to be distracted from what you've lost and fixed and saved by somebody. Which is pretty banal" (PK 498).

If the world can't satisfy us, then the next best thing is to be distracted. Desire co-opts distraction as its most dependable Plan B. Faced with the user-unfriendliness of the real, we want to be distracted and entertained. So much of the real is dull and indifferent and expensive. The cost of the real feels too high and so we dream about something else, something easier, someplace else. We may sit down in our office chairs but, when we do, we're like Hal who, though he's managed to sit down, spends his time "scrolling through an alphabetical list of the faraway places he'd rather be" (IJ 806). We prefer exotic maps of imaginary places to the dull terrain of real bodies.

We run from the dull like death itself. Why is it that "dullness proves to be such a powerful impediment to attention" (PK 85)? What's so terrifying about an empty room or a silent car or a hard math problem? Why does boredom seem painful? Shouldn't it just be boring?

> Maybe dullness is associated with psychic pain because something that's dull or opaque fails to provide enough stimulation to distract people from some other, deeper type of pain that is always there, if only in an ambient low-level way, and which most of us spend nearly all our time and energy to distract ourselves from feeling, or at least from feeling directly or with our full attention. ... surely something must lie behind not just Muzak in dull or tedious places anymore but now also actual TV in waiting rooms, supermarkets' checkouts, airports' gates, SUVs' backseats. Walkmen, iPods, BlackBerries, cell phones that attach to your head. This terror of silence with nothing diverting to do. I can't think anyone really believes that today's so-called "information society" is just about information. Everyone knows it's about something else, way down. (PK 85)

Dullness is not itself the problem. Dullness just fails to mask the problem: an immaturity that, because it believes in heads rather than bodies, suffers the circularity of a self-confirming despair. Distraction is a defensive measure. We're desperate to be diverted and most anything shiny will do.

# 10

# Watching

Picture Joe Briefcase, Wallace's hypothetical average American. And now picture Joe watching (what was in 1993) the national average of six hours of TV per day. This is a serious investment in distraction. "Six hours a day is more time than most people (consciously) do any other one thing. How human beings who absorb such high doses understand themselves will naturally change, become vastly more spectatorial, self-conscious" (SF 34). Distraction, rather than being occasional and derivative, becomes perpetual and primary. Rather than being a diversion from the main thing you do, it becomes the main thing you do. Unavoidably, then, the self gets fitted to its work. With all that watching, the body gets gradually reduced to a head and the head gets gradually reduced to a pair of eyes. People get shaped into watchers who, when they turn their attention back to the world, have a hard time not getting looped into the habit of just watching themselves watching. "The practice of 'watching' is expansive. Exponential" (SF 34). It's self-amplifying.

Gripping entertainment is a prosthesis for the head that boosts the head's involutions while outsourcing responsibility for its content. TV is built to be user-friendly and its easiness is at the heart of its appeal. Unlike other causes to which we might give our lives, TV generates the illusion that it asks for little in return. "Television's greatest minute-by-minute appeal is that it engages without demanding. One can rest while undergoing stimulation. Receive without giving" (SF 37). TV offers the illusion of lively company and access to vibrant, exotic locations. But in truth, it offers only outlines and schemata. It doesn't connect us with solid people and bodies and places. It connects us with frictionless images of people and bodies and places. "It's ultimately of course not even actors we're espying, not even people: it's EM-propelled analog waves and ion streams and rear-screen chemical reactions throwing off phosphenes in grids of dots" (SF 24). And, more, "the dots are coming out of our *furniture*, all we're really spying on is our own *furniture*" (SF 24).

What does it mean if Joe Briefcase daily devotes six hours of rapt attention to a piece of furniture? What does it mean if the most vibrant connection in his life is with a TV screen? "Television resembles certain other things one might call Special Treats (e.g. candy, liquor), i.e. treats that are basically fine and fun in small amounts but bad for us in large amounts and *really* bad for us if consumed in the massive regular amounts reserved for nutritive staples" (SF 37). Joe's investment of six hours a day is likely more than sufficient to reach that tipping point where the world, rather than being a measure for the head, gets measured by the head as wanting. As a distraction machine, TV feeds the head's closed loop. It feeds the head's hope for an exit plan. "Television purveys and enables *dreams*, and most of these dreams involve some sort of transcendence of average daily life" (SF 39). TV engineers a prosthetic transcendence that is more than passingly similar to our dreams about the kind of transcendent release that religion should promise.

> The modes of presentation that work best for TV—stuff like "action," with shoot-outs and car wrecks, or the rapid-fire collage of commercials, news, and music videos, or the "hysteria" of prime-time soap and sitcom with broad gestures, high voices, too much laughter—are unsubtle in their whispers that, somewhere, life is quicker, denser, more interesting, more … well, *lively* than contemporary life as Joe Briefcase knows it. This might seem benign until we consider that what good old average Joe Briefcase does more than almost anything else in contemporary life is watch television, an activity which anyone with an average brain can see does not make for a very dense and lively life. (SF 39, ellipsis original)

In this way, TV offers a double indictment of the real. It proposes an unrealistic measure for real life (real life *should* be full of the kind of always bright, funny, supernaturally beautiful people that are engineered for TV) while simultaneously situating a piece of wired furniture at the heart of Joe's real life. TV whispers in his ear, "Joe, Joe, there's a world where life is lively, where nobody spends six hours a day unwinding before a piece of furniture" and then follows this up with the non sequitur, "Joe, Joe, your best and only access to this world is TV" (SF 39).

The ease and user-friendliness of TV comes with real costs. TV offers an existential loan that is riddled with hidden fees and backloaded with balloon payments. "As a Treat, my escape from the limits of genuine experience is neato. As a steady diet, though, it can't help but render my own reality less attractive (because in it I'm just one Dave, with limits and restrictions all over the place), render me less fit to make the most of it (because I spend all my time pretending I'm not in it), and render me ever more dependent on the device that affords escape from just what my escapism makes unpleasant" (SF 75).

Investing that much time in staring at the world through an electric fiction of a pane of glass, we end up carrying the pane of glass around with us even when we're not watching TV. The glass shapes us into a certain kind of self, a self that's suited to the glass, a self that can't quite touch the world in front of it for all the glass that's protecting it from the world. The self gets defined as a watcher, as a viewer, as a witness. "We spend enough time watching, pretty soon we start watching ourselves watching. Pretty soon we start to 'feel' ourselves feeling, yearn to experience 'experiences'" (SF 34). Our contact with the real gets doubled and mediated and spaced by a loop of self-conscious watching. We become the boy who's watched so much porn that he can't have sex, he can only watch himself trying to have sex. The human weight of the act gets pushed back from the experience itself, back behind the camera lens, to the now isolated observation of the experience.

When this happens, we stop driving cars and, instead, wonder how we look driving cars. We stop wearing clothes and, instead, wonder how we look wearing clothes. "For 360 minutes per diem, we receive unconscious reinforcement of the deep thesis that the most significant quality of truly alive persons is watchableness, and that genuine human worth is not just identical with but *rooted in* the phenomenon of watching" (SF 26). It's an inevitable consequence of investing so much time in watching. Watching and watchability become the measure of value and significance. We spend our time watching movies with witty banter and pulsing soundtracks and then when we leave the couch to go somewhere ourselves we double the experience with a stream of music, photos, texts, updates, and ironic self-commentary. We start to look like the camera-infatuated man Wallace meets on his cruise:

> This sad and cadaverous guy, who by the second day I'd christened Captain Video, has tall hard gray hair and Birkenstocks and very thin hairless calves, and is one of the cruise's most prominent eccentrics. Pretty much everybody on the *Nadir* qualifies as camera-crazy, but Captain Video camcords absolutely *everything*, including meals, empty hallways, endless games of geriatric bridge—even leaping onto Deck 11's raised stage during Pool Party to get the crowd from the musicians' angle. You can tell that the magnetic record of Captain Video's Megacruise experience is going to be this Warholianly dull thing that is exactly as long as the Cruise itself. (SF 307–308)

Captain Video, come his journey's end, will have exactly doubled his cruise ship experience with his videotaping of that experience—except that, as a result of this doubling, he won't have experienced a cruise at all. He'll only have experienced himself recording what *would* have been a cruise if he hadn't spent all his time recording it. His consolation is that when he gets home, he'll get to watch all that watching a second time.

# 11

# Assassins

Remy Marathe is wheelchair bound. And French-Canadian. And a terrorist. But his wife is dying, he needs help caring for her, and so he has agreed to work for the United States Office of Unspecified Services (U.S.O.U.S.) as a double agent. (Unless, of course, it's just a stunt and he's actually functioning as a triple agent. Or even a quadruple agent. Such scenarios probably aren't mutually exclusive.) Marathe lost his legs the same way all the members of his terrorist organization have: he won the train-jumping game. The game is played by lining up six boys alongside some train tracks and then waiting for a train to come. As the train barrels toward them, each boy must jump the track. The first boy to jump loses. The last boy to jump wins and proves his mettle. The trouble is that the winners often jump so late that they also lose their legs in the process. The end result, though, is a whole cadre of tough, willful, committed terrorists who, because they've proven themselves, are all confined to wheelchairs.

The United States, the wheelchair assassins believe, has been hollowed out by its addiction to distraction and entertainment and, at this late hour, it needs only a little push to complete its implosion. This is why the assassins are scrambling to track down a Master cartridge of the lethally entertaining film "Infinite Jest." In a conversation with a U.S.O.U.S. agent, Hugh Steeply, Marathe explains why their plan is so dangerous and why Americans, even if warned, won't be able to keep from watching the film. In his broken and careless English, Marathe explains that we won't be able to stop ourselves because now is what has happened when a people choose nothing over themselves to love, each one. A U.S.A. that would die—and let its children die, each one—for the so-called perfect Entertainment, this film. Who would die for this chance to be fed this death of pleasure with spoons, in their warm houses, alone, unmoving. Hugh Steeply, in complete seriousness as a citizen of your neighbor I say to you: forget for a moment the Entertainment, and think instead about a U.S.A. where such a thing could be possible enough for your Office to fear: can such a U.S.A. hope to survive for a much longer time? (IJ 318)

Our love of distraction is killing us. The problem isn't the master cartridge but the people who "would die for this chance to be fed this death of pleasure with spoons, in their warm houses, alone, unmoving." The real problem isn't the choice but our willingness to choose it.

We've reached the point where our addiction to distraction has become malignant. This, Wallace argues, is why "the analogy between television and liquor is best" (SF 38). TV isn't evil in itself. But then neither is alcohol. TV "may become malignantly addictive only once a certain threshold of quantity is habitually passed, but then the same is true of Wild Turkey" (SF 38). "An activity is addictive if one's relationship to it lies on that downward-sloping continuum between liking it a little too much and really needing it. Many addictions, from exercise to letter-writing, are pretty benign. But something is *malignantly* addictive if (1) it causes real problems for the addict, and (2) it offers itself as a relief from the very problems it causes" (SF 38). An addiction moves from benign to malignant when, like a cancer, the addiction starts to spread and repurpose life for its own sake rather than being one part of that life. When the addiction acquires an entrenched, institutional, bureaucratic aspect that displaces the self and cares for little more than its own preservation and extension, then the head has begun to metastasize. The key moment is when the addiction becomes circular, when the addiction starts offering itself as a solution to the very problems it's causing. If you drink because you're angry and disappointed and drinking in turn makes you even more angry and disappointed, then the circle has closed. "What looks like the cage's exit is actually the bars of the cage"

(IJ 222). The addiction is ramping up. Your pursuit of transcendence is robbing you of transcendence. "In a case such as this," Marathe warns, "you become the slave who believes he is free. The most pathetic of bondage" (IJ 108).

This answer to the problem of worship doesn't attempt to satisfy desire so much as kill it. The abused Substance substitutes itself "for something nourishing and needed, and the original genuine hunger—less satisfied than bludgeoned—subsides to a strange objectless unease" (SF 39). If life refuses to be easy and user-friendly, then whatever *is* easy and user-friendly can at least be used to fight our way out of life. Here, the addiction to some Substance again gets intertwined with an addiction to thinking. And, due to its very character, an addiction to thinking is not the kind of thing you can think your way out of. The "interior psychic worm"—the worm that twists everything around to serve the addiction itself—turns too fast for that (IJ 200). The integrity of thinking has been compromised and something else will have to intervene.

Consider what happens when you try to just think your way through to an important decision.

> In an intentional bout of concentrated major thinking, where you sit down with the conscious intention of confronting major questions like *"Am I currently happy?"* or *"What, ultimately, do I really care about and believe in?"* or—particularly if some authority figure has just squeezed your shoes—*"Am I essentially a worthwhile, contributing type of person or a drifting, indifferent, nihilistic person?,"* then the questions often end up not answered but more like beaten to death, so attacked from every angle and each angle's different objections and complications that they end up even more abstract and ultimately meaningless than when you started. Nothing is achieved this way, at least that I've heard of. Certainly, from all evidence, St. Paul, or Martin Luther, or the authors of *The Federalist Papers*, or even President Reagan never changed the direction of their lives this way—it happened more by accident. (PK 191)

Nothing fundamental gets changed this way. At that level of abstraction, everything stays abstract. It stays stuck in the head.

Questions don't get answered like this, they get beaten into a gray quiescence. If something else—something redemptive and road-to-Damascus-like—is going to happen, it will have to start in the body rather than in the head.

# 12

# Irony

Irony colludes with abstraction. It facilitates distraction. It greases the head's wheels and keeps them spinning. It helps us pretend we're not spending six bodiless hours a day staring at a piece of furniture. Irony is a defensive posture and, as a defense mechanism, it's built right in as a basic feature of our culture of distraction. TV, by shaping us into watchers, primes us for an irony that keeps the world at a safe distance. "'Television,' after all, literally means 'seeing far'; and our six hours daily not only helps us feel up-close and personal at like the Pan-Am Games or Operation Desert Shield but also, inversely, trains us to relate to real live personal up-close stuff the same way we relate to the distant and exotic, as if separated from us by physics and glass, extant only as performance, awaiting our cool review" (SF 64). Being ironic, we can point at bodies and laugh without admitting our own embodiedness. We can treat life itself as a spectacle staged for our entertainment and then roll our eyes when it insists on being ordinary and user-unfriendly.

    TV consciously invests in the cultivation of irony because irony keeps us watching. We can "watch" TV ironically without, then, really watching it. It's easier to take the work of distraction seriously if we ironically distract ourselves from the seriousness of our investment. "Given that television must revolve off basic antinomies about being and watching, about escape from daily life, the averagely intelligent viewer can't be all that happy about his daily life of high-dose watching. Joe Briefcase might have been happy enough *when* watching, but it was hard to think he could be too terribly happy *about* watching so much" (SF 58). Irony helps manage this tension between the excitement TV offers and the obvious role that its distraction plays in making our own lives duller. TV resolves this tension by presenting itself as essential, graduate-level training in the kind of ironic watching that will empower us to absorb the repercussions of watching so much TV.

> And to the extent that it can train viewers to laugh at characters' unending put-downs of one another, to view ridicule as both the mode of social intercourse and the ultimate art-form, television can reinforce its own queer ontology of appearance: the most frightening prospect, for the well-conditioned viewer, becomes leaving oneself open to others' ridicule by betraying passé expressions of value, emotion, or vulnerability. Other people become judges; the crime is naïveté. The well-trained viewer becomes even more allergic to people. Lonelier. Joe B's exhaustive TV-training in how to worry about how he might come across, seem to watching eyes, makes genuine human encounters even scarier. But televisual irony has the solution: further viewing begins to seem almost like required research, lessons in the blank, bored, too-wise expression that Joe must learn how to wear for tomorrow's excruciating ride on the brightly lit subway, where crowds of blank, bored-looking people have little to look at but each other. (SF 63)

Lonely and bored, we watch TV. This in turn makes our lives more boring and lonely. To protect ourselves from this irony, we become ironic.

In order to keep us watching (in order to make us even better, more disciplined, more enduring watchers), TV tutors us in how to respond to life itself with a defensive, "numb blank bored demeanor—what one friend calls the 'girl-who's-dancing-with-you-but-would-obviously-rather-be-dancing-with-somebody-else' expression—that has become my generation's version of cool" (SF 64). This ironic posture, this cool deportment, becomes your default expression. You may be dancing with someone, but you're not *really* dancing with them. You may show up at work, but you're not *really* working. You keep your distance. You're kind of here, but really you'd rather be someplace else with someone else. Irony practices a "coolness" that watches (and critiques and mocks and comments) without getting involved.

Hal Incandenza's brother, Mario, was severely deformed at birth. As a result, his head is disproportionately big, his arms are largely useless, he's strapped into a complicated brace, and when he walks he tilts at a forty-five degree angle to the floor. Wallace describes Mario as having "khaki-colored skin, an odd dead gray-green that in its corticate texture and together with his atrophic in-curled arms and arachnodactylism gave him, particularly from a middle-distance, an almost uncannily reptilian/dinosaurian look" (IJ 314). Appearance-wise, he is anything but cool. But, more importantly, he's not cool in that he doesn't keep his distance from what's happening. Mario, like Drinion, has an uncanny ability to just be where he is. As a result,

> his younger and way more externally impressive brother Hal almost idealizes Mario, secretly. God-type issues aside, Mario is a (semi-) walking miracle, Hal believes. People who're somehow burned at birth, withered or ablated way past anything like what might be fair, they either curl up in their fire, or else they rise. Withered saurian homodontic Mario floats, for Hal. He calls him Booboo but fears his opinion more than probably anybody except their Moms's. Hal remembers the unending hours of blocks and balls on the hardwood floors of early childhood's 36 Belle Ave., Weston MA, tangrams and See 'N Spell, huge-headed Mario hanging in there for games he could not play, for make-believe in which he had no interest other than proximity to his brother. (IJ 316–317)

Mario, though always on the margins of the book's plot, may be the closest thing *Infinite Jest* has to a hero. "The older Mario gets," Wallace tells us, "the more confused he gets about the fact that everyone at E.T.A. over the age of about Kent Blott finds stuff that's really real uncomfortable and they get embarrassed. It's like there's some rule that real stuff can only get mentioned if everybody rolls their eyes or laughs in a way that isn't happy" (IJ 592). TV enforces this rule: talk about nothing that's really real without distance, eye-rolling, and plenty of commercial breaks.

# 13

## Masks

Wallace imagines a future where videophones become common. And he imagines, with hilarious precision, the catastrophic chain of events that would follow. The trouble starts when people immediately begin to regret the loss of privacy a videophone entails. Where you used to talk on the phone without giving any thought to your appearance, now every phone call is like welcoming a stranger into your living room. More, it is no longer possible to pretend to be giving a caller your full attention. "Video telephony rendered the fantasy insupportable. Callers now found they had to compose the same sort of earnest, slightly overintense listener's expression they had to compose for in-person exchanges" (IJ 146).

An arms race of techniques for improving one's appearance ensues. The solution "was, of course, the advent of High-Definition Masking" (IJ 147).

> Mask-wise, the initial option of High-Definition Photographic Imaging—i.e. taking the most flattering elements of a variety of flattering multi-angle photos of a given phone-consumer and—thanks to existing image-configuration equipment already pioneered by the cosmetics and law-enforcement industries—combining them into a wildly attractive high-def broadcastable composite of a face wearing an earnest, slightly overintense expression of complete attention—was quickly supplanted by the more inexpensive and byte-economical option of (using the exact same cosmetic-and-FBI software) actually casting the enhanced facial image in a form-fitting polybutylene-resin mask. (IJ 148)

The long-term problems that follow are obvious. The better the masks become, the more distance people put between themselves and the image they project to the world. The image takes on a life of its own and the mask-wearers become a function of the mask.

> In a gradually unsubtilizing progression, within a couple more sales-quarters most consumers were now using masks so undeniably better-looking on videophones than their real faces were in person, transmitting to one another such horrendously skewed and enhanced masked images of themselves, that enormous psychosocial stress began to result, large numbers of phone-users suddenly reluctant to leave home and interface personally with people who, they feared, were now habituated to seeing their far-better-looking masked selves on the phone and would on seeing them in person suffer (so went the callers' phobia) the same illusion-shattering aesthetic disappointment that, e.g., certain women who always wear makeup give people the first time they ever see them without makeup. (IJ 148–149)

The mask is a defensive gesture. It's meant to give you enough space to breathe easily. But, instead, the mask buries you beneath layers of cool, enhanced beauty, insulating you from contact with anything but schemata.

The mask is like a commercial. Or, better, it's a like a commercial that pretends to be art, because the mask doesn't present itself as a mask but as a face. It doesn't present itself as a paid advertisement but as a friend.

> An ad that pretends to be art is—at absolute best—like somebody who smiles warmly at you only because he wants something from you. This is dishonest, but what's sinister is the cumulative effect that such dishonesty has on us: since it offers a perfect facsimile or simulacrum of goodwill without goodwill's real spirit, it messes with our heads and eventually starts upping our defenses even in cases of genuine smiles and real art and true goodwill. It makes us feel confused and lonely and impotent and angry and scared. It causes despair. (SF 289)

It's not TV itself (or the masks, or the ads) that's the problem. It's the cumulative effect. It's the way they mess with our heads, shape our expectations, and keep us defensive. It's the way the mask presents itself as a solution to the very problem it's feeding. We feel lonely and unloved and so we try to make ourselves more attractive and so we end up prisoners behind our own masks feeling lonelier than ever. The temptation, then, to no one's surprise, is to double-down on the problem and commission an even better mask. Hell is this malignant recursivity: masks on top of masks. Hell is a world full of masks without faces, of heads without bodies.

In *The Pale King*, Lane Dean, Jr. ends up working for the IRS because, with a wife and child to support, he needs a job with decent pay and benefits. Early in the novel, Dean and his future wife, just teenagers, are sitting on a picnic table by a lake. She's pregnant and they have to decide whether to keep the baby. Sitting beside her, Dean doesn't know what to do. Analysis paralysis sets in. "Sitting here beside this girl as unknown to him as outer space, waiting for whatever she might say to unfreeze him, now he felt like he could see the edge or outline of what a real vision of hell might be" (PK 41). Hell, Dean discovers, looks like two masked armies, silent, facing each other but never battling. "The armies stay like that, motionless, looking across at each other and seeing therein something so different and alien from themselves ... frozen like that, opposed and uncomprehending, for all human time" (PK 41). Hell is this strange, blank hypocrisy that knows neither itself nor the other. It's this kind of loneliness that can't even admit what it's "really lonely for: this hideous internal self, incontinent of sentiment and need, that pulses and writhes just under the hip empty mask" (IJ 695).

Your only hope is to set down the masks and come back to your user-unfriendly body. But this is hard to do. The head is so appealing and the mask so tempting. To avoid getting trapped behind masks, you'll need some good training, some bad luck, or, most likely, a healthy dose of both. You'll need the kind of misfortune that befell Edward Rand, Meredith's husband. Edward has been sick for a long time, since before Meredith met him, but he doesn't like to talk about his health. When Meredith asks about his health, he always brushes off her questions. "All he'd say was that his health was a mess but that the advantage of being a physical mess was that he looked exactly as much of a mess as he really was, there was no way to hide it or pretend he was less of a mess than he felt like" (PK 490). In this sense, Edward's bad luck is lucky. He can't get his mask to work and, so, he's spared the trouble of living with one.

# 14

# Beauty

Joelle Van Dyne ties together *Infinite Jest*'s three plot lines. Joelle was in love with Hal Incandenza's brother, Orin. She starred in many of their father's films and is rumored, notably, to be featured in the film "Infinite Jest." As Madame Psychosis, late-night radio show host, she is adored by Hal's brother, Mario. After an attempted drug overdose, she ends up in the Ennet Recovery and Halfway House, down the hill from the tennis academy, under the supervision of Don Gately. Eventually, she's pursued by the wheelchair assassins. It's no surprise that Joelle attracts so much attention. Wallace describes her in all seriousness as "the P.G.O.A.T., for the Prettiest Girl Of All Time" (IJ 290). Hiding behind a veil that covers her face, she tells Don Gately:

> Don, I'm perfect. I'm so beautiful I drive anybody with a nervous system out of their fucking mind. Once they've seen me they can't think of anything else and don't want to look at anything else and stop carrying out normal responsibilities and believe that if they can only have me right there with them at all times everything will be all right. Everything. Like I'm the solution to their deep slavering need to be jowl to cheek with perfection. (IJ 538)

It's never entirely clear why Joelle starts wearing a veil. Most likely, her face was disfigured by an accident involving acid. But it could be that she's too beautiful not to wear one. It could just be that her beauty is too hard for people. She strikes others as the walking embodiment of a shining, breathing, uppercase Substance. If only they could have her, surely they would finally be satisfied. This illusion is too much to bear. Ironically, rather than being a magnet for men, it turns out that "she was almost universally shunned" because she "induced in heterosexual males what U.H.I.D. later told her was termed the Actaeon Complex, which is a kind of deep phylogenic fear of transhuman beauty" (IJ 290). Joelle, after all, is "almost grotesquely lovely" (IJ 290).

Beauty attracts because it's user-friendly. As Drinion tells Rand, "It's almost always pleasant to pay attention to beauty. It requires no effort" (PK 456). And, in general, it takes way less beauty than the transdimensional kind Joelle wields to set the worship-ready head's full range of fantasies in motion. As a recovering addict, Gately sees clearly how susceptible his head is to such fantasies. He recognizes that his powerful attraction to Joelle (even veiled) is just a ramped up version of what's *always* going on in his head.

> If a halfway-attractive female so much as smiles at Don Gately as they pass on the crowded street, Don Gately, like pretty much all heterosexual drug addicts, has within a couple blocks mentally wooed, shacked up with, married, and had kids by that female, all in the future, all in his head, mentally dandling a young Gately on his mutton-joint knee while this mental Mrs. G bustles in an apron she sometimes at night provocatively wears with nothing underneath. (IJ 862)

This tendency to prioritize beauty, Wallace argues, gets exaggerated by our investment in TV. Shaped as watchers, watchability becomes especially important. "When everybody we seek to identify with for six hours a day is pretty, it naturally becomes more important to us to be pretty, to be viewed as pretty. Because prettiness becomes a priority for us, the pretty people on TV become all the more attractive, a cycle which is obviously great for TV" (SF 53). The problem is that this turns out to be "less great for us civilians, who tend to own mirrors, and who also tend not to be anywhere near as pretty as the TV-images we want to identify with" (SF 53).

Joelle's beauty, though not technically a mask, still ends up working like one. Joelle joins the Union of the Hideously and Improbably Deformed (U.H.I.D.) because, increasingly, she feels a deep need to hide. U.H.I.D., though, rather than teaching her *not* to hide, helps her stop hiding her need to hide. According to this line of thought, wearing a veil is itself a form of disclosure. When you refuse to wear a veil "what you do is *hide* your deep need to hide, and you do this out of the need to *appear* to other people as if you have the strength not to care how you *appear* to others" (IJ 535). In short, "you take your desire to hide and conceal it under a mask of acceptance" (IJ 535). So, "the veil's a way to not hide" your desire to hide (IJ 536). Appearance, whether it's deformed or transhumanly perfect, can work as a mask.

 Meredith Rand also sees how being beautiful both gives her power and takes that power away. Beauty is a type of power, she says, in that "you get treated special, and people pay attention to you and talk about you, and if you walk in someplace you can almost feel the room change" (PK 481–482). But it's also a kind of trap "because the power you have is all totally connected to prettiness, and at some point you realize that the prettiness is like a kind of box you're always in, or prison, that nobody's ever going to see you or think about you apart from the prettiness" (PK 482). Beauty, like success, is no uppercase Substance. It can't solve your problems or save you from desire.

# 15

# Time

To mask her pain, Joelle starts using cocaine. Before she overdoses, nearly dies, and ends up in recovery at Ennet House, she tries to quit several times. Each time she fails because time itself turns out to be too much. Or, to be more precise, the way she experiences time—not discretely but cumulatively—is too much. Instead of living time through her body's grounded connection with the present, she does what most of us do: she lives time through her head and then gets crushed by the head's insistence on living the past, present, and future all at once. But the present is too fragile and fleeting to support all that weight.

Trying to quit cocaine, "I'd bunker up all white-knuckled and stay straight," Joelle tells Gately. "And count the days. I was proud of each day I stayed off. Each day seemed evidence of something, and I counted them. I'd add them up. Line them up end to end. You know?" (IJ 859). Hanging on to what's passed, Joelle wants her numbered days of sobriety to be evidence of something, to prove something about her—or, really, to hide something about her. She strings the days together like pearls she can wear, like a magic talisman that proves that she, as a human being, is okay. This is what the head does best: it counts, it adds, it calculates, it hoards, it multiplies, it proves things to itself. The trouble is that "soon it would get … improbable. As if each day was a car Knievel had to clear. One car, two cars. By the time I'd get up to say like maybe about 14 cars, it would begin to seem like this staggering number. Jumping over 14 cars. And the rest of the year, looking ahead, hundreds and hundreds of cars, me in the air trying to clear them" (IJ 859, ellipsis original). Who can live this way? The head is too small. Time is too full. "Who could do it? How did I ever think anyone could do it that way?" (IJ 859).

Hal Incandenza describes a similar experience of "telescopically self-conscious panic" (IJ 896). He felt time telescope outward in both directions as "the familiarity of Academy routine took on a crushing cumulative aspect" (IJ 896). First, the past refuses to pass. "The total number of times I'd schlepped up the rough cement steps of the stairwell, seen my faint red reflection in the paint of the fire door, walked the 56 steps down the hall to our room, opened the door and eased it gently back flush in the jamb to keep from waking Mario. I reexperienced the year's total number of steps, movements, the breaths and pulses involved" (IJ 896–897). The head insists on not just experiencing but reexperiencing time. (One breath at a time is fine. But who can breathe a whole year's worth of air?) And then, second, a crush of possible futures arrives all at once.

> Then the number of times I would have to repeat the same processes, day after day, in all kinds of light, until I graduated and moved away and then began the same exhausting process of exit and return in some dormitory at some tennis-power university somewhere. Maybe the worst part of the cognitions involved the incredible volume of food I was going to have to consume over the rest of my life. Meal after meal, plus snacks. Day after day after day. Experiencing this food in toto. Just the thought of the meat alone. One megagram? Two megagrams? (IJ 897)

But the specificity of this vision is what, in the end, makes it so terrifying:

> I experienced, vividly, the image of a broad cool well-lit room piled floor to ceiling with nothing but the lightly breaded chicken fillets I was going to consume over the next sixty years. The number of fowl vivisected for a lifetime's meat. The amount of hydrochloric acid and bilirubin and glucose and glycogen and gloconol produced and absorbed and produced in my body. And another, dimmer room, filled with the rising mass of the excrement I'd produce, the room's double-locked steel door gradually bowing outward with

the mounting pressure .... I had to put my hand out against the wall and stand there hunched until the worst of it passed. (IJ 897, ellipsis original)

The repetition is horrifying, the weight of a lifetime's worth of working and eating and shitting. Even if Hal gets what he wants and plays for some tennis-power university somewhere, he'll still have to sleep and wake and dress and brush his teeth and eat (again) and shit (again) and run his drills and complete his homework. On and on. The accumulation of time reveals the vanity of his head's hopes for something different, for some kind of apocalyptic completion. "I look at these guys," Hal says, "that've been here six, seven years, eight years, still suffering, hurt, beat up, so tired, just like I feel tired and suffer, I feel this what, dread, this dread, I see seven or eight years of unhappiness every day and day after day of tiredness and stress and suffering stretching ahead, and for what, for a chance at a like a pro career that I'm starting to get this dready feeling a career in the Show means even *more* suffering" (IJ 109). The price of life is steep. And our longed-for futures can't arrive without first submitting to the restrictions and taxes imposed by the present. No matter when we are, there's no place to be but now.

# 16

# Deskwork

The nature of the head's problem with telescoping time is clear to the addict. But it also becomes painfully clear to Lane Dean Jr. when he starts working for the IRS. His new middle-class desk job with government benefits seemed like a boon, but once there he starts to see what the job actually entails: a desk, a chair, a pencil, some memos, some forms, an unending stream of tax returns in need of examination, and a clock. Especially the clock. The job doesn't ever finish, it just takes breaks. Coffee breaks, lunch breaks, night breaks, weekend breaks. But the number of returns waiting to be examined, with all their columns and numbers and deductions, never decreases. Dean tries to stop himself from thinking about this, but "try as he might he could not this last week help envisioning the inward lives of the older men to either side of him, doing this day after day. Getting up on Monday and chewing their toast and putting their hats and coats on knowing what they were going out the door to come to for eight hours. This is boredom beyond any boredom he'd ever felt. This made the routing desk at UPS look like a day at Six Flags" (PK 377). Imagining the inner lives of these other men, treating them as avatars of his future self, is not a good idea. It is, again, a way of piling up time, of cramming decades of work into the next half hour before his afternoon break.

In the course of Dean's eight-hour days, his short breaks start to assume an outsized importance. But the more important his breaks become, the less he's able to enjoy them. One day, Dean distractedly follows two other guys outside for some air, but once he's out there he sees that he "hasn't come outside with the other two; he just happened to step out for air on the break at the same time" (PK 122). He doesn't really know what he's doing. "He's still looking for a really desirable, diverting place to go during breaks; they're too important" (PK 122). Sitting outside, he watches the other two chat in a relaxed way. Dean, though, can't relax at all. In fact, returning to work may turn out to be a relief because sitting here, watching the seconds of his break drain away, "Lane Dean is starting now to feel desperate about the fact that the break's fifteen minutes are ticking inexorably away and he is going to have to go back in and examine returns for another two hours before the next break" (PK 123). How will he manage the next two hours? Let alone the next two years?

Dean tries using some of the relaxation techniques recommended by his trainers.

> Lane Dean Jr. with his green rubber pinkie finger sat at his Tingle table in his Chalk's row in the Rotes Group's wiggle room and did two more returns, then another one, then flexed his buttocks and held to a count of ten and imagined a warm pretty beach with mellow surf as instructed in orientation the previous month. Then he did two more returns, checked the clock real quick, then two more, then bore down and did three in a row, then flexed and visualized and bore way down and did four without looking up once except to put the completed files and memos in the two Out trays side by side up in the top tier of trays where the cart boys could get them when they came by. After just an hour the beach was a winter beach, cold and gray and the dead kelp like the hair of the drowned, and it stayed that way despite all attempts. (PK 376)

Dean's head can't get him out of this problem because his head is the problem. He can't deal with the desperation generated by his wanting to be someplace else by *more* effectively imagining that he's someplace else. That image of a pretty beach with mellow surf is what's ratcheting up his despair. It's no cure for it. Dean's head is desperate to stay out of the present, but the user-unfriendly reality of the present is a gravity well sucking him back in. Dean tries to focus and do "another one, then a plummeting inside of him as the wall clock showed that what he'd thought was another hour had not been. Not even close. 17 May 1985. Lord Jesus Christ have mercy on me a poor sinner" (PK 377). Seated at his tax return examination desk trying to scan through another return, Lane Dean Jr. gets religion instead. As time's horizon gradually contracts to a small black point of disappointed, fantasy-free, present-tense hopelessness, he spontaneously prays. Lord Jesus Christ have mercy on me a poor sinner!

We fear this compression of time, this contraction of the head's wide range of hopeful possibilities to the raw fact of the present's actual body. Having bought the lie that the head is freedom and that fantasy is liberty (having mistaken the bars of the cage for its exit), we fear the present like a prison. Adrift at sea on his Caribbean cruise, Wallace reports a parallel moment of recognition and contraction.

> I am now 33 years old, and it feels like much time has passed and is passing faster and faster every day. Day to day I have to make all sorts of choices about what is good and important and fun, and then I have to live with the forfeiture of all the other options those choices foreclose. And I'm starting to see how as time gains momentum my choices will narrow and their foreclosures multiply exponentially until I arrive at some point on some branch of all life's sumptuous branching complexity at which I am finally locked in and stuck on one path and time speeds me through stages of stasis and atrophy and decay until I go down for the third time, all struggle for naught, drowned by time. (SF 267–268)

Part of what Wallace's luxury cruise is selling is pampered relief from this burden of responsibility, from his responsibility to make adult choices and willingly surrender the other futures that, as a result, get foreclosed. The cruise is selling the fantasy of a victory over time's inevitable contraction—now or later—to the simplicity of the present. But the present, no matter how hard the head fights to get beyond it, is the only body the head will ever have. Committing to the present *is* a kind of death, but the other choice is worse. "To experience commitment as the loss of options, a type of death, the death of childhood's limitless possibility, of the flattery of choice without duress—this will happen, mark me. Childhood's end. The first of many deaths" (PK 228). If you never surrender that abstract freedom and commit to the limitation of something real, the crucial revelation will never dawn. You'll fail to discover that such commitments aren't just a kind of dying, they're the substance of life. Life *is* this contraction of open possibilities into an irrevocable actuality. Life passes, from the very start, as the work of dying.

# 17

# Sewage

The head is restless. It has trouble sitting still. And this is true regardless of pleasure or circumstance. There is, as Wallace notes of himself, some "ur-American part of me that craves and responds to pampering and passive pleasure: the Dissatisfied Infant part of me, the part that always and indiscriminately WANTS" (SF 316). This dissatisfaction presents as a human-shaped hole. The creeping despair that overtakes Wallace on his Caribbean cruise follows from how the cruise systematically brings the entire entertainment-satisfaction-industrial complex to bear on filling this hole. His despair is generated partly by the impossibility of their succeeding but, more, his despair is also generated by how successful the cruise *is*, with all its well-funded machinations, at relieving him of the very thing that makes him human.

The cruise ship's commitment to cabin cleaning epitomizes much of the ambivalence that's been fueling Wallace's despair. Whenever he leaves his room for more than thirty minutes—and Wallace stages a whole series of comic experiments to precisely determine the time frame—his cabin, no matter how disheveled, is inspection-ready when he returns. The ship's attention to detail strikes him as almost motherly. This is a pleasant effect, but it's also troubling.

> I submit that there's something deeply mind-fucking about the Type-A personality service and pampering on the *Nadir*, and that the manic invisible cabin-cleaning provides the clearest example of what's creepy about it. Because, deep down, it's not *really* like having a mom. *Pace* the guilt and nagging, etc., a mom cleans up

after you largely because she loves you—you are the point, the object of the cleaning somehow. On the *Nadir*, though, once the novelty and convenience have worn off, I begin to see that the phenomenal cleaning has nothing to do with me. (SF 298–299)

Wallace's worry becomes especially pointed when it acquires a bit more specificity:

(It's been particularly traumatic for me to realize that Petra is cleaning Cabin 1009 so phenomenally well simply because she is under orders to do so, and thus (obviously) that she's not doing it for me or thinks I'm No Problem or A Funny Thing—in fact, she'd clean my cabin just as phenomenally well even if I were a dork—and maybe conceivably behind the smile does consider me a dork, in which case what if in fact I really am a dork?—I mean, if pampering and radical kindness don't seem motivated by strong affection and thus don't somehow affirm one or help assure one that one is not, finally, a dork, of what final and significant value is all this indulgence and cleaning?) (SF 299)

A luxury cruise messes with your head. On the one hand, it offers the promise of care, relaxation, and satisfaction. But on the other hand, it only offers these things as a paid service. It both aims to meet your deepest personal needs and only to meet them out of a sense of impersonal, contractual obligation.

This smarts especially, for Wallace, in terms of the personal connection he feels to Petra, his beautiful cabin steward. Is she cleaning the cabin for *him*? Yes and no. She does clean up after him but not as the result of any personal care for him. Wallace wants her actions to offer him some reassurance that he's not a dork, that he's not lacking, that he's not a human-shaped hole. And he despairs when it turns out that her cabin-cleaning can't offer this reassurance because the cruise's luxury only *simulates* care. Petra gets compared to a mom on this score. A mother will clean up after you, but her motivations are different. A mother's care may reassure you when it comes to your being a dork but, unlike the cruise, it's not because she's sure that you *aren't* a dork. Rather, with your mother, it's a reassurance that comes from the fact that her care is a response to your dorkiness. Her reassurance stems from her willingness to care for the dork that you are, not from the mutually agreed upon fantasy that—wink-wink, here's $5000—you aren't one.

Recognizing this, Wallace is now in a position to appreciate what he calls "the lie at the dark heart of Celebrity's brochure" (SF 316). The "central fantasy the brochure is selling" is "the promise to sate the part of me that always and only WANTS" (SF 316). But that dissatisfied infant part of us isn't going away. It can't be purged without purging life itself.

> The thing to notice is that the real fantasy here isn't that this promise will be kept, but that such a promise is keepable at all. This is a big one, this lie. And of course I want to believe it—fuck the Buddha—I want to believe that maybe this Ultimate Fantasy Vacation will be *enough* pampering, that this time the luxury and pleasure will be so completely and faultlessly administered that my Infantile part will sated. But the Infantile part of me is insatiable. (SF 316–317)

The big lie, of course, is not that the cruise could keep this promise but that such a promise is keepable at all.

The cruise ship fantasy comes to a head in Wallace's terrifying description of cabin 1009's astonishingly powerful toilet:

> But all this is still small potatoes compared to 1009's fascinating and potentially malevolent toilet. A harmonious concordance of elegant form and vigorous function, flanked by rolls of tissue so soft as to be without the usual perforates for tearing, my toilet has above it this sign:
>
> THIS TOILET IS CONNECTED TO A **VACUUM SEWAGE SYSTEM**. PLEASE DO NOT THROW INTO THE TOILET ANYTHING THAN [sic] ORDINARY TOILET WASTE AND TOILET PAPER
>
> Yes that's right a *vacuum toilet*. And, as with the exhaust fan above, not a lightweight or unambitious vacuum. The toilet's flush produces a brief but traumatizing sound, a kind of held high-B gargle, as of some gastric disturbance on a cosmic scale. Along with this sound comes a concussive suction so awesomely

powerful that it's both scary and strangely comforting—your waste seems less removed than hurled from you, and hurled with a velocity that lets you feel as though the waste is going to end up someplace so far away from you that it will have become an abstraction ... a kind of existential-level sewage treatment. (SF 304–305, ellipsis original)

This is baseline human fantasy. The fantasy we're being sold (again and again) is of an "existential-level sewage treatment." This is a sewage treatment that not only removes your waste but denies with its sheer concussive force that you had any in the first place. "You are not full of shit," it repeats reassuringly, "you are *not* full of shit." The treatment is meant to reassure you that you are not a dork and that life is not insatiable. It's a fantasy built on an industrial-grade response to the lack that defines you, to your inability to keep what you've eaten, to the impossibility of ingesting the world and achieving a final satisfaction. And, more, it's a response that turns, ultimately, on denying a basic fact of life: its passing. Bodies are organs of passing. To deny this passing and the shit that passes through you is to deny the body itself. It's the same old story the head is always trying to tell.

Nothing more clearly compromises our idolatry than excrement. Nothing more clearly attests to the passage of time and the inversion of transcendence. Shit is the idol disenchanted. It's proof of disappointment. It's what follows on the far side of desire, on the flipside of the Möbius loop's turning. It shows the nature of life's passing and displays how transcendence and immanence continually traverse just one single surface. Shit is the world inassimilable. It's the world displayed not as an object that might satisfy but, instead, as something beyond your ability to keep and control, beyond possession altogether. Shit is life liberated, it's the world "sacred, on fire with the same force that lit the stars" (TW 93).

# 18

## Size

These are adult truths. They're too big to fit just in your head. To absorb them, you'll need your body too. The work, though, is not impossible. In many ways, it's disarmingly simple. You're already doing it. In a late section of *The Pale King*, an intern claims to have learned these truths "at just twenty-one or twenty-two, at the IRS's Regional Examination Center in Peoria, where I spent two summers as a cart boy" (PK 437). Even work as a cart boy may be enough to clear room in your head. Having gotten so far, so early, the boy is identified as lifetime Service material. "This, according to the fellows who saw me as fit for a Service career, put me ahead of the curve, to understand this truth at an age when most guys are starting only to suspect the basics of adulthood—that life owes you nothing; that suffering takes many forms; that no one will ever care for you as your mother did; that the human heart is a chump" (PK 437).

The basic truth of adulthood is the opposite of what you thought when you were a child. When you were a child you thought that being an adult meant that you would finally be big. But the door swings the other way. Being an adult means discovering that you're actually way smaller than you'd guessed. You had no idea. We don't like to think about it but it's pressingly obvious: "our smallness, our insignificance and mortality, yours and mine, the thing that we spend all our time not thinking about directly, that we are tiny and at the mercy of large forces" (PK 143). Large force number one is time. We don't want to see that "time is always passing and that every day we've lost one more day that will never come back and our childhoods are over and our adolescence and the vigor of youth and soon our adulthood, that everything we see around us all the time is decaying and passing, it's all passing away, and so are we, so am I" (PK 143). But this is not all, it's not just us. "Everybody who knows me or even knows I exist will die, and then everybody who knows those people and might even conceivably have even heard of me will die, and so on, and the gravestones and monuments we spend money to have put in to make sure we're remembered, these'll last what—a hundred years? two hundred?—and they'll crumble" (PK 143). Within just "three or four generations it will be like I never existed, not only will I have passed away but it will be like I was never here" (PK 143). But there is no reason to stop here. The conflagration is much bigger. "Everything is on fire, slow fire, and we're all less than a million breaths away from an oblivion more total than we can even bring ourselves to even try to imagine, in fact, probably that's why the manic US obsession with production, produce, produce, impact the world, contribute, shape things, to help distract us from how little and totally insignificant and temporary we are" (PK 143–144).

# 19

# Silence

Mr. DeWitt Glendenning Jr. is the Director of the IRS's Midwest Regional Examination Center. Glendenning claims that if you know the position a person takes on taxes, you can determine their whole philosophy (PK 82). Taxes are the dividing line. The direction you break in relation to the world's user-unfriendly resistance is decisive. When it's time to sit down and go to work, what do you do? How many diversions do you entertain? How many fantasy beaches do you visit? Is your work a distraction from your head's more important business of fantasizing about some uppercase Substance? Or are your head's fantasies a distraction from the ordinary work?

Chris Fogle, erstwhile nihilist but eventual catechumen of the IRS, finds that treating life itself as a distraction has a deadening effect. "I never seem to recognize important moments at the time they're going on—they always seem like distractions from what I'm really supposed to be doing" (PK 217–218). Dreaming about the dramatic, Fogle treats what's real as a distraction from his dreams. Hal Incandenza suffers from the same. When he joins others in a room, "he's aware that they sense he's somehow there only in a very technical sense, that he's got an air of moment's-notice readiness to leave about him" (IJ 703). Hal's head can't sit. It just flits. And heads that flit convey the impression that their bodies, though present, are not really there. Even if the body stays, the head has already left the room. You know the routine:

> The way hard deskwork goes is in jagged little fits and starts, brief intervals of concentration alternated with frequent trips to the

men's room, the drinking fountain, the vending machine, constant visits to the pencil sharpener, phone calls you suddenly feel are imperative to make, rapt intervals of seeing what kinds of shapes you can bend a paperclip into, & c. This is because sitting still and concentrating on just one task for an extended length of time is, as a practical matter, impossible. (PK 291)

Or, at least, depending on the head, it seems impossible.

While on an orientation tour of the Examination Center in Peoria, the fictional David Wallace's guide accidentally opens a heavy door to a room full of IRS examiners arranged in long rows of desks, bent over their work. The room is charged with silence. "This silence I remember best of all, because it was both sensuous and incongruous. For obvious reasons, we tend to associate total quiet with emptiness, not with large groups of people" (PK 290). Just one glimpse of that room left Wallace both elated and terrified. "In hindsight, I know that there was something about the silent, motionless intensity with which everyone in that opened door's instant was studying the tax-related documents before them that frightened and thrilled me. The scene was such that you just knew that if you were to open the door for another brief instant ten, twenty, or forty minutes later, it would look and sound just the same. I had never seen anything like it" (PK 290). Wallace is gripped by an envy that simultaneously repels and attracts him.

> Seeing this was kind of traumatic. I'd always felt frustrated and embarrassed about how much reading and writing time I actually wasted, about how much I sort of blinked in and out while trying to absorb or convey large amounts of information. To put it bluntly, I had felt ashamed about how easily I got bored when trying to concentrate. As a child, I think I'd understood the word *concentrate* literally and viewed my problems with sustained concentration as evidence that I was an unusually dilute or disorganized form of human being, and laid much of the blame for this on my family, who tended to need a lot of loud noise and distraction going on at all times and undertook almost every kind of activity with every available radio, stereo, and television set on, such that I'd taken to wearing special high-filter customized ear plugs at home from the

age of fourteen on. It took me all the way up to the age of finally getting away from Philo and entering a highly selective college to understand that the problem with stillness and concentration was more or less universal and not some unique shortcoming. (PK 292)

This peek into silence crystallizes for Wallace what it means to be human and it reveals the possibility of a grounded intensity he hadn't yet suspected.

Gerhardt Schtitt, the tennis academy's head coach, drills this into his young athletes: "The true opponent, the enfolding boundary, is the player himself. Always and only the self out there, on court, to be met, fought, brought to the table to hammer out terms" (IJ 84). The contest is always the same. "You compete with your own limits to transcend the self in imagination and execution. Disappear inside the game: break through the limits: transcend" (IJ 84). This, though, is a weird kind of transcendence. It's one thing to disappear, distracted, *from* the game. This is the head's specialty. This is a typical kind of transcendence that just involves the head's refusal to be local. But in this scenario, in this silent-room-full-of-electric-desks scenario, the transcendence involves disappearing *into* the game, *into* the work. Rather than leaving the world, the head, transcending itself, rejoins it.

# 20

# Immersion

Hal Incandenza's oldest brother, Orin, is a professional football player, a punter. Like Hal, he attended the Enfield Tennis Academy. Orin was good enough to easily land a tennis scholarship at Boston University but not nearly good enough to make a serious run at the Show. His specialty was the lob. When Orin first meets Joelle Van Dyne, she's a cheerleader for BU's football team. While there's not a man there who can take his eyes off her, no one has the guts to talk to her. Orin stumbles onto the football field, hoping to bump into her and, when a football rolls his way, he picks it up and "accidentally" kicks it with some truly spectacular height, distance, and accuracy. His pro-quality lobbing of tennis balls finds a perfect analog in what's required for the pro-quality punting of footballs. BU's football coach knows a star when he sees one. Orin gives up tennis, joins the football team, and starts dating Joelle.

Orin comes to love the purity of punting. On the field in a massive stadium with all eyes on him, Orin experiences a capacity for concentration and connection that is profoundly lacking in the rest of his life. Punting, Orin is free. "Orin's back against Delaware, ready, his helmet a bright noncontact white and his head's insides scrubbed free for ten seconds of every thought not connected to receiving the long snap and stepping martially forward to lob the leather egg beyond sight at an altitude that makes the wind no factor" (IJ 299). Ten seconds of freedom. Ten seconds with his head scrubbed clean and his concentration whole and his body zeroed in on exactly what's happening here and now. This is Orin's version of levitation, "what happens when he is completely immersed" (PK 485).

But the public dimension of Orin's experience is hard to replicate. His own laser-like concentration in that moment is fed by the intense focus of thousands of other people. But what about the rest of life? Is it possible to bring this same liberating attention to eating breakfast, to driving in traffic, to examining tax returns? Orin becomes a football hero as a result of his specialized skill set. But professional football is only played once a week, and that for just four or five months a year. And the punter is only on the field punting for a handful of seconds each game. That's too little for a life. The between-time is the thing. "To retain care and scrupulosity about each detail from within the teeming wormball of data and rule and exception and contingency which constitutes real-world accounting—this is heroism" (PK 231). That kind of connection depends on learning how to pay attention to life's insignificant details. It depends on learning how to care for their errancy and opacity. It depends on bringing yourself to bear on what presents as boring, again and again, until you finally discover "that boring activities become, perversely, much less boring if you concentrate intently on them" (IJ 203).

This is Drinion's discovery. This is why he can dial-in and levitate. Meredith Rand asks him, is "paying attention the same thing as being interested in somebody?" And Drinion responds: "Well, I would say almost anything you pay close, direct attention to becomes interesting" (PK 456). But the only way to discover this is to attend. In attending, even to something that's boring and user-unfriendly, the polarity of the experience can get reversed. Instead of the head supplying the juice and investing objects with attraction, the objects themselves, seen with care and attention, start to exert a magnetic pull. Given a chance, ordinary objects can exert a tractor-beam of counter-intentionality that, unlike the head's small investment, draws on the world's own vast network of interlocking power grids.

This switch in the experience's power source from the head to the world depends on our ability to slow down. Mario, Hal's handicapped brother, is capable of this same Drinion-like attention. "Hal's brother is, technically, Standford-Binet-wise, slow, the Brandeis C.D.C. found—but *not*, verifiably *not*, retarded or cognitively damaged or bradyphrenic, more like refracted, almost, ever so slightly epistemically bent, a pole poked into mental water and just a little off and just taking a little bit longer, in the manner of all refracted things"

(IJ 314). Mario's head takes just a little bit longer and, as a result, his whole experience of the world gets refracted. This refraction gives the world time to exert some of its own pull before Mario's attention can run off, looking for something else to worship that might be more interesting or satisfying. That little bit of time is enough to change what's boring into something interesting, to take what's hard and connect him to it.

Joelle reaches a turning point in her own struggle with addiction when she sits helpless at Don Gately's hospital bedside long enough to feel the same thing. Sitting there—just sitting there—by his bed watching him, "it's the first time she's felt sure she wants to keep straight no matter what it means facing" (IJ 710). Keeping the line between the head and the body open depends on this willingness to put down our maps and face the real. Doing so, the real can give itself in some refracted way. It can give itself as something to which the head belongs. The hard things are right in front of us. They've been with us all along, overlooked. The opaque, the painful, the boring, the unjust: "try to learn to let what is unfair teach you" (IJ 174). Try to listen. "It's all educational. How promising you are as a Student of the Game is a function of what you can pay attention to without running away" (IJ 176).

Attention can be trained. Given a chance, the world can tutor your capacity to concentrate. It can plug your head back into your body with its welter of feelings and sensations. These sensations aren't all pleasant, but they are all live. When you go into a recovery program, people will reassure you and "tell you how it'll all get better and better as you abstain and recover" (IJ 446). But what "they somehow omit to mention" is that some of these feelings hurt, "that the way it gets better and you get better is through pain. Not around pain, or in spite of it" (IJ 446).

This problem arises immediately. Trying to feel your way back into the sensitive fingers and toes of your body, you'll remember how sensitive they are, how open to feelings of all kinds. And you'll remember that this sensitivity, like a sore tooth, was why your head took flight in the first place. "They neglect to tell you that after the urge to get high magically vanishes and you've been Substanceless for maybe six or eight months, you'll begin to 'Get In Touch' with why it was that you used Substances in the first place. You'll start to feel why it was you got dependent on what was, when you get right down to it, an anesthetic" (IJ 446). Paying attention, you willingly set the head's anesthesia aside. You stop sleeping through your own life. You stop hiding in distractions. And, then, when you do, the head will click back into the body, the wire will go live, and the feelings and sensations will start, in all their great variety, to pour through.

# 21

# Indifference

Turning life's tap back on requires a kind of courage that is committed to whatever comes. It depends on the kind of indifference that Joelle models when she decides she wants to stay straight no matter what that means facing. This is a funny kind of indifference. It's a kind of indifference whose polarity has also been reversed. Stuck in our heads, we're indifferent to whatever hard or user-unfriendly things come along. But when the tide turns—when the head slows down and attention increases—then, instead of being indifferent to the world, we open ourselves to it by practicing a kind of indifference toward the head. Chris Fogle sees the distinction between these two types of indifference in himself and his father. His father, an accountant, had learned to say "'Whatever' to his lot in life, but obviously in a different way from the way in which the directionless wastoids of my generation said 'Whatever'" (PK 192). The first "whatever" is a way of saying "yes" to the world, come what may. The second "whatever"—the nihilistic "whatever" of a directionless wastoid—is the head's way of saying "no" to life but "yes" to itself.

The conversion of one type of indifference into the other turns on an experience of "acceptance" that is less a function of the head finally figuring things out than of the head's surrender. At least at first, "'acceptance' is usually more a matter of fatigue than anything else" (IJ 204). There is a kind of forced recognition that

> both destiny's kisses and its dope-slaps illustrate an individual person's basic personal powerlessness over the really meaningful

events in his life: i.e. almost nothing important that ever happens to you happens because you engineer it. Destiny has no beeper; destiny always leans trenchcoated out of an alley with some sort of *Psst* that you usually can't even hear because you're in such a rush to or from something important you've tried to engineer. (IJ 291)

This recognition comes as a kind of death. It's the death of the head's dream of independence and sufficiency. It's the death of Substance abuse. When you live through this death and your head becomes indifferent to itself—and, thus, open again to worlds and bodies—you may, ironically start to look dead to others. For instance, "certain people find people like Mario Incandenza irritating or even think they're outright bats, dead inside in some essential way" (IJ 156). While wrong in the most important sense, this intuition is right in another. Mario is different because he *is* dead in some essential way. His fantasy pursuit of an uppercase Substance has withered and died. He's lost track of his idols. His head's apparitions have dried up. "Mario, like Lyle, tends to take data pretty much as it comes" (IJ 379). "Everything he sees hits him and sinks without bubbles" (IJ 128). Similarly, Rand asks Drinion: "You like the work?" Drinion thinks about this for a minute and says: "I think I don't like it or dislike it either" (PK 450).

This positively charged and weirdly alive indifference is liberating. It doesn't add up to an indifference to life but to an indifference to the head's own typical indifference to anything other than itself. This positive indifference, no longer paralyzed by fear, puts the ball back in play. Ted Schacht, an older student at the tennis academy, has had this kind of "acceptance" and freedom forced on him by injuries.

> Schacht always prefers a pleasant match, one way or the other. He really doesn't care all that much whether he wins anymore, since first the Crohn's and then the knee at sixteen. He'd probably now describe his desire to win as a preference, nothing more. What's singular is that his tennis seems to have improved slightly in the two years since he stopped really caring. It's like his hard flat game stopped having any purpose beyond itself and started feeding on itself and got fuller, looser, its edges less jagged. (IJ 266)

With his head clear, Schacht is free to play tennis. And that freedom to play has improved his game. His game's been liberated by a kind of hopelessness that recognizes the impossibility of getting the idol his head was searching for. His game has passed through the furnace of despair and come out the far side with an enlivening honesty and credibility. "Pat told Gately that grim honesty and hopelessness were the only two things you need to start recovering from Substance-addiction, but that without these qualities you were totally up the creek" (IJ 464). But with these two things, a previously impossible effectiveness opens up. Chris Fogle's substitute accounting professor gives off this same vibe of hopeless, indifferent, and effective candor.

> He was not anxious to "connect" or be liked. But nor was he hostile or patronizing. What he seemed to be was "indifferent"—not in a meaningless, drifting, nihilistic way, but rather in a secure, self-confident way. It's hard to describe, although I remember the awareness of it very clearly. The word that kept arising in my mind as he looked at us and we all watched and waited—although all of this took place very quickly—was *credibility*. (PK 226)

From the outside, it's possible to confuse this kind of credibility with nihilism. But from the inside, the difference is stark. The credibility of a hopelessness that has given itself back to the work of paying attention is the kind of honesty that's capable of love.

# 22

# Boredom

Boredom is a head-clearing ascesis. And, as an ascesis, it can be practiced. You can practice sitting still or staring at a wall or not reading on the toilet. The key to clearing your head is "to find the other side of the rote, the picayune, the meaningless, the repetitive, the pointlessly complex. To be, in a word, unborable" (PK 438). Finding the other side of boredom is empowering. "If you are immune to boredom, there is literally nothing you cannot accomplish" (PK 438).

Though unfinished, *The Pale King* includes an appendix with a selection of Wallace's working notes. The notes sketch some of the different directions the plot might have taken. One note regarding Drinion says:

> Drinion is *happy*. Ability to pay attention. It turns out that bliss—a second by second joy + gratitude at the gift of being alive, conscious—lies on the other side of crushing, crushing boredom. Pay close attention to the most tedious thing you can find (tax returns, televised golf), and, in waves, a boredom like you've never known will wash over you and just about kill you. Ride these out, and it's like stepping from black and white into color. Like water after days in the desert. Constant bliss in every atom. (PK 546)

Some hyperbole creeps in here, but the impulse is sound. There is something that happens on the other side of boredom, on the far side of transcendence, after the head clears and some silence gathers. And this thing is connected to an awareness of life and consciousness per se, to a recognition of attention as such, rather than just consciousness of idol X, idol Y, or idol Z. And, perhaps most importantly, this thing that happens involves a temporal contraction that shifts the scale of our experience from months and weeks to minutes and seconds.

Wallace plays with this idea in a description he gives of Toni Ware's childhood. Ware's childhood is rough and unstable. Her "mom was a bit nuts, as was her own mom, who was a notorious recluse and eccentric who lived in the Hubcap House in Peoria" (PK 439). Ware is dragged by her mom from place to place and boyfriend to boyfriend. Along the way, it's Ware's doll that loses its body and carries on as just an unthreaded head. We're told that "both the mom and the grandmother had been given to catatonic/cataleptic states, which as far as I can tell is a symptom of a certain kind of schizophrenia" (PK 439). It's in the margins of this illness that Ware herself will explore the far side of boredom:

> The girl, ever since young, had amused herself by trying to imitate this [catatonic] state, which involved sitting or lying extremely still, slowing your pulse, breathing in such a way that your chest doesn't even rise, and holding your eyes open for long periods, such that you're blinking only every couple minutes. It's the last that's hardest—the eyes start to burn as they dry out. Very, very hard to push through this discomfort … but if you do, if you can resist the almost involuntary urge to blink that comes when the burning and the drying is the very worst, then the eyes will start lubricating themselves without blinking. They will manufacture a kind of false or ersatz tears, just to save themselves. Almost no one knows this, because the incredible discomfort of having your eyes open without blinking stops most people before they hit the critical point. (PK 439–440, ellipsis original)

If you can resist the head's almost involuntary urge to run away, the polarity can change and the experience can open up. Most of us don't know this because we blink. We succumb to distraction. We check our phones or queue up another show.

Another anonymous interviewee for the "Your IRS Today" documentary (#917229047) gives a parallel description. He wants to write a play about being a tax examiner that would "be a totally real, true-to-life play" (PK 106). However, the more true-to-life the play is, the more unperformable it becomes. "It would be unperformable, that was part of the point" (PK 106). The play works like this: "The idea's that a wiggler, a rote examiner, is sitting poring over 1040s and attachments and cross-filed W-2s and 1099s and like that. The setting is very bare and minimalistic—there's nothing to look at except this wiggler, who doesn't move" (PK 106). The play continues on like this, with the examiner just examining forms, "until the audience gets more and more bored and restless, and finally they start leaving, first just a few and then the whole audience, whispering to each other how boring and terrible the play is" (PK 106). As entertainment, the play offers no distraction. It fails as a prosthetic for the head. But "then, once the audience have all left, the real action of the play can start" (PK 106). The play enacts, in miniature, the arc Wallace has in mind. It dramatizes a willingness to patiently and persistently face the real, tax return after tax return, until the audience in your head gets bored and leaves. Once this happens, the real action of the play can begin. Once life is no longer conducted as an entertaining diversion for the head, the body is free to feel, think, and act.

The transition involved here is something like the shift from watching something half-baked and fuzzy on your TV to being aware that you're a body sitting on a couch watching a piece of furniture. Christ Fogle, as an undergrad, gets hooked on daytime soaps. One day, watching *As the World Turns*, Fogle notices how, after every commercial break, the "network announcer's voice would say, '*You're watching* As the World Turns', which he seemed, on this particular day, to say more and more pointedly each time" (PK 222). The announcer repeats the phrase again and again "until the tone began to seem almost incredulous—'*You're watching* As the World Turns'— until I was suddenly struck by the bare reality of the statement. I don't mean any humanities-type ironic metaphor, but the literal thing he was saying" (PK 222). The bare truth of it strikes like lightning and Fogle wakes up from distraction to find himself in the world. "It could not have felt more concrete if the announcer had actually said, '*You're sitting on an old yellow dorm couch, spinning a black-and-white soccer ball, and watching* As the World Turns, *without ever even acknowledging to yourself this is what you are doing*'" (PK 222). The shift in perspective is small but stark. Fogle wakes up to discover what's been true all along, to see what's been right in front of him. He doesn't wake up to some other world. He just wakes up to the fact that he's *in* a world. Fogle says, "The truth is I was not even aware of the obvious double entendre of '*You're watching* As the World Turns' until three days later—the show's almost terrifying pun about the passive waste of time sitting there watching something whose reception through the hanger didn't even come in very well, while all the while real things in the world were going on and people with direction and initiative were taking care of business in a brisk and no-nonsense way" (PK 222). Boredom's revelation works like this double entendre. It takes a cliché you've heard a thousand times and then shows you a substantial meaning you'd never seen before. What had been black and white starts playing in color.

# 23

# Awareness

Fogle was primed for this epiphany by his recreational experience with a drug called Obetrol. Obetrol was originally sold as a diet pill in the 1950s and '60s. In the '90s, the pill was reformulated; its name was changed to Adderall and it was marketed as a treatment for Attention Deficit Disorder. Obetrol gave Fogle an artificial peak at the possibility of a life that wasn't Substance-driven. Obetrol showed him—however momentarily and synthetically—what the other side of boredom looked like. It functioned as "a kind of signpost or directional sign, pointing to what might be possible if I could become more aware and alive in daily life" (PK 186). As a college student, he tells us, I "was basically so feckless and unfocused during this period that I needed a very clear, blunt type of hint that there was much more to being an alive, responsible, autonomous adult than I had any idea of at the time" (PK 186). Obetrol put him in a position to appreciate the freedom that a life devoted to taxes offered.

Obetrol showed Fogle that "awareness is different from thinking" (PK 190). Where thinking is focused on map-making and map-reading, awareness is focused on the terrain. This new focus made him aware of where he was. It moved him from just watching as the world turned to being aware that he was watching as the world turned. Under the bright light of awareness, a fog lifted and a whole world of tiny details, complex relationships, and nested contexts revealed themselves.

> *I am in this room right now. The shadow of the foot is rotating on the east wall. The shadow is not recognizable as a foot because*

> of the deformation of the angle of the light of the sun's position behind the sign. I am seated upright in a dark-green easy chair with a cigarette burn on the right armrest. The cigarette burn is black and imperfectly round. The track I am listening to is 'The Big Ship' off of Brian Eno's Another Green World, *whose cover has colorful cutout figures inside a white frame.* (PK 182)

The trouble with a description like this is that, once translated into words, it sounds like more thinking. But that would miss the point. What this awareness really "felt like was a sort of emergence, however briefly, from the fuzziness and drift of my life in that period. As though I was a machine that suddenly realized it was a human being and didn't have to just go through the motions it was programmed to perform" (PK 182).

Obetrol didn't juice up Fogle's experience of the world and make "colors brighter and music more intense" (PK 182). Rather, "what became more intense was my awareness of my own part in it, that I could pay real attention to it" (PK 182). It revealed the possibility of attention. And it didn't make everything feel pleasant or good. It just made things real and present. "Nor was it just good or pleasurable things you were aware of .... Some of the stuff it brought into awareness wasn't pleasant, it was just reality" (PK 184). This awareness was indifferent to the head's preference (or not) for the object and, as a result, it could care about the details of the object's reality regardless.

As a shortcut, Obetrol couldn't do more than offer a glimpse of what some other life might be like. The awareness it offered was temporary "and after I came off of the Obetrol—which usually involved a bad headache—afterward, I felt as though I barely remembered any of the things I'd become aware of. The memory of the feeling of suddenly coming awake and being aware felt vague and diffuse" (PK 185). Without the Obetrol, Fogle's brief interval of awareness is itself reduced to a vague and fuzzy map. The drug opened a doorway out of his head and showed him the view but then, before he could walk through, it slammed the door shut again. "But there was no denying it was powerful—the feeling that everything important was right there and I could sometimes wake up almost in mid-stride, in the middle of the meaningless bullshit, and suddenly be aware of it" (PK 187).

# 24

# Heroes

The big question isn't whether it's possible to live after we die. The question is whether it's possible to live, now, in a 3' × 3' cubicle. Can a body breathe there? Can it feel there? Can it live there? Or is the only real choice left to climb into your head and pull the ladder up after you? I'm not sure about the cubicle, but I'm increasingly confident that I can't go on living in my head.

One of the most arresting and enigmatic characters in all of Wallace's fiction is *The Pale King*'s Jesuit priest. Chris Fogle, adrift in college, is struggling to pull his life together. Studying feverishly for an exam on the *Federalist Papers* and aiming to attend one final review session, he doesn't notice until it's too late that he's landed in the wrong room. Instead of American Political Thought, he's in a final review for an Advanced Tax course. A substitute is conducting this final review, a Jesuit priest whose name we're never told. "He was slender, and in the room's bright lighting he looked pale in a way that seemed luminous" (PK 217). For attire, "he wore an archaically conservative dark-gray suit whose boxy look might have been actual flannel, and his dress shoes' shine was dazzling" (PK 215). "He seemed lithe and precise; his movements had the brisk economy of a man who knows that time is a valuable asset" (PK 215). When this man entered the room, the "room's whole voltage changed" (PK 217). He had the bearing of a war veteran.

As the Jesuit begins his review with the help of carefully prepared and projected transparencies, Fogle felt "a sort of electric coolness in [his] head" (PK 218). The review was conducted briskly and efficiently. It was "rapid, organized, undramatic, and dry in the way of people who know that what they are saying is too valuable in its own right to cheapen with concern about delivery" (PK 219). It is, for Fogle, a classic conversion experience. He's about to find Jesus. He discovers that his freedom to be ironic and nihilistic and avoid, at every turn, any kind of taxing commitment, is not freedom but a prison. He'd mistaken the bars of the cage for its exit. "If I wanted to matter—even just to myself—I would have to be less free, by deciding to choose in some kind of definite way" (PK 224). He would have to give up the free-floating freedom of his head and tether himself back to the taxing constraints of some particular body in some particular place.

When the bell rings and the review ends, no one gets up to leave. "When the substitute turned from raising the screen, he gave none of the bodily signals of completion or transition to final instructions or summary. He stood very still—noticeably stiller than most people stand when they stand still" (PK 225). Then he said to the class: "All right, then. Before you leave here to resume that crude approximation of a human life you have heretofore called a life, I will undertake to inform you of certain truths" (PK 227). Riveted, Fogle records the following:

> This may be the first time you've heard the truth put plainly, starkly. Effacement. Sacrifice. Service. To give oneself to the care of others' money—this is effacement, perdurance, sacrifice, honor, doughtiness, valor. Hear this or not, as you will. Learn it now, or later—the world has time. Routine, repetition, tedium, monotony, ephemeracy, inconsequence, abstraction, disorder, boredom, angst, ennui—these are the true hero's real enemies, and make no mistake, they are fearsome indeed. For they are real. (PK 231)

> Here is a truth: Enduring tedium over real time in a confined space is what real courage is. Such endurance is, as it happens, the distillate of what is, today, in this world neither I nor you have made, heroism. (PK 229)

> Not heroism as you might know it from films or the tales of childhood. You are now nearly at childhood's end; you are ready for the truth's weight, to bear it. The truth is that the heroism of your childhood entertainments was not true valor. It was theater.

The grand gesture, the moment of choice, the mortal danger, the external foe, the climactic whose outcome resolves all—all designed to appear heroic, to excite and gratify an audience. An audience. (PK 229)

Gentlemen, welcome to the world of reality—there is no audience. No one to applaud, to admire. No one to see you. Do you understand? Here is the truth—actual heroism receives no ovation, entertains no one. No one queues up to see it. No one is interested. (PK 229)

True heroism is *a priori* incompatible with audience or applause or even the bare notice of the common run of man. (PK 230)

The less conventionally heroic or exciting or adverting or even interesting or engaging a labor appears to be, the greater its potential as an arena for actual heroism, and therefore as a denomination of joy unequaled by any you men can yet imagine. (PK 230)

True heroism is you, alone, in a designated work space. True heroism is minutes, hours, weeks, year upon year of the quiet, precise, judicious exercise of probity and care—with no one there to see or cheer. This is the world. Just you and the job, at your desk. (PK 230)

When he's done, the priest gathers his things and leaves. And then Fogle does, too.

# 25

# Revelations

**B**oredom's revelation, like the US tax code, is hidden in plain view. No one's concealed anything from the public. "The reason for this public ignorance is not secrecy. Despite the IRS's well-documented paranoia and aversion to publicity, secrecy here had nothing to do with it" (PK 83). What, then, is the problem? "The real reason why US citizens were/are not aware of these conflicts, changes, and stakes is that the whole subject of tax policy and administration is dull. Massively, spectacularly dull" (PK 83). Life hides behind a sheen of dullness. Its familiarity buffers our relationship. Attention, generally galvanized only by what might feed the head's daydreams, slides right off the world at our feet.

But a hopeless head is in a position to learn. It may wake up to the world as it turns. It may decide to join the Service and, serving, learn something about the user-unfriendly. David Wallace says of his time working for the IRS: "I learned, in my time with the Service, something about dullness, information, and irrelevant complexity. About negotiating boredom as one would a terrain, its levels and forests and endless wastes. Learned about it extensively, exquisitely, in my interrupted year" (PK 85).

Those who learn to negotiate this terrain become prophets and seers. They walk the earth as revelators, seeing the real at every turn. They become data mystics. Claude Sylvanshine is a seer and the prosaic keeps revealing itself to him.

An obscure but true piece of paranormal trivia: There is such a thing as a *fact psychic*. Sometimes in the literature also known as a *data mystic*, and the syndrome itself as *RFI* (= *Random-Fact Intuition*). These subjects' sudden flashes of insight or awareness are structurally similar to but usually far more tedious and quotidian than the dramatically relevant foreknowledge we normally conceive as ESP or precognition. This, in turn, is why the phenomenon is so little studied or publicized, and why those possessed of RFI almost universally refer to it as an affliction or disability. In what few reputable studies and monographs exist, examples nonetheless abound; indeed, abundance, together with irrelevance and the interruption of normal thought and attention, composes the essence of RFI phenomenon. (PK 118)

Not unlike Mario, the data-mystic suffers from what looks like a curse or disability, from revelatory interruptions that refract their perceptions of the world and slow down the rushing, inward screwing spin of their thoughts.

*The Pale King* claims that there's good empirical evidence and scientific documentation for the existence of the fact psychic, but nobody cares. The ability seems pointless. Everything it reveals is tedious. It only brings into focus what's irrelevant to the head's projects. "The fact psychic lives part-time in the world of fractious, boiling minutiae that no one knows or could be bothered to know even if they had the chance to know" (PK 120). The fact psychic may spontaneously and intuitively know things like "the metric weight of all the lint in all the pockets of everyone at the observatory in Fort Davis TX on the 1974 day when a scheduled eclipse was obscured by clouds" (PK 120). In this kind of revelation, the heavens literally stay closed. A spectacular eclipse goes unseen. But the lint in people's pockets comes into precise focus. Or, it may be the case that the fact psychic "tastes a Hostess cupcake" and then "knows where it was made; knows who ran the machine that sprayed a light coating of chocolate frosting on top; knows the person's weight, shoe size, bowling average, American Legion career batting average; he knows the dimensions of the room that person is in right now. Overwhelming" (PK 121).

This kind of skill won't help you make it big. Rather than making you special, it will confirm your ordinariness. Rather than being a practical advantage in your pursuit of a Substance, it will create drag and slow things down. If you've developed this ability to perceive minutiae, don't try to use to get ahead. "Datum: at least one-third of ancient ruler's seers and magicians were in fact fired or killed early in their tenure because it emerged that the bulk of what they foresaw or intuited was irrelevant. Not incorrect, just irrelevant, pointless" (PK 119).

# 26

# Abiding

Don Gately is an addict. Demerol is his poison of choice. But Gately is also a recovering addict; he's an addict who's *aware* he's an addict. And that subtle difference, that small diffraction, is the whole ballgame. It's the difference between life and death.

Physically, Gately is a mountain. Rooms part around him. He can barely squeeze behind the wheel of a car. Worried about his aging bulk, he does crunches at the foot of his bed. He lives and works at the Ennet halfway house as a resident staffer, steering other addicts through the onset of recovery. Back in the day, to feed his enormous habit, he worked in the margins of organized crime. He collected gambling debts. He stole high-end electronics. He was a deft burglar. He has, unwittingly, killed people. Among other things, the DA is still after him for murder. Further, by all reports, his cooking is terrible. And now Gately is afraid that, in the middle of trying to right his life, he may be, in a highly inappropriate move, falling in love with the halfway house's newest resident, Joelle van Dyne.

*Infinite Jest*'s second battle royale occurs outside the halfway house, right around midnight. Some big Canadians, fresh from a late-night luau, are looking for the sadistic addict that killed their dog. Gately is forced to intervene and, with a pro linebacker's size and agility, puts them all down with his bare hands—but only after taking a bullet himself. Gately lands in the hospital in desperate need of pain medication. But he refuses any drugs. He's fought too long and too hard to risk a relapse. If he falls back into that hole, he may never climb out again.

In order to deal with the pain, Gately will have to get very serious about the recovering addict's classic mantra: one day at a time.

Like Joelle, he'll have to stop living time in big chunks and, instead, allow the scope of his life to contract. You have to "build a wall around each individual 24-hour period and not look over or back. And not to count the days. Even when you get a chip for 14 days or 30 days, not to add them up" (IJ 858). The head has to stop adding things up and, instead, let life pass as it actually comes, single file. Anything more is "too much to think about" (IJ 860). No matter how fierce the pain gets, the thing that's "unendurable is what his own head could make of it all. What his head could report to him, looking over and ahead and reporting. But he could choose not to listen: he could treat his head like ... clueless noise. He hadn't quite gotten this before now, how it wasn't just the matter of riding out the cravings for a Substance" (IJ 860–861). But the truth is that "everything unendurable was in the head, was the head not Abiding in the Present but hopping the wall and doing a recon and then returning with unendurable news that you then somehow believed" (IJ 861).

This isn't the first time Gately's been forced to do something like this, to rein the head in and make it sit. In the past, though, he didn't have a choice. Tossed into jail, he was forced to greet the pain of an abrupt detox face first.

> Gately remembered some evil fucking personal detoxes ... Cold Turkey. Abrupt Withdrawal. The Bird. Being incapable of doing it and yet having to do it, locked in. A Revere Holding cage for 92 days. Feeling the edge of every second that went by. Taking it a second at a time. Drawing the time in around him real tight. Withdrawing. Any one second: he remembered: the thought of feeling like he'd be feeling this second for 60 more of these seconds—he couldn't deal. He could not fucking deal. He had to build a wall around each second just to take it. The whole first two weeks of it are telescoped in his memory down into like one second—less: the space between two heartbeats. A breath and a second, the pause and gather between each cramp. An endless Now stretching its gull-wings out on either side of his heartbeat. And he'd never before or since felt so excruciatingly alive. Living in the Present between pulses. What the White Flaggers talk about: living completely In The Moment. (IJ 859–860)

Stuck in the hospital, Gately will have to do the same thing. But this time he'll have to do it of his own volition. He'll have to personally tell the doctors, through the rasp of the plastic tube stuck down his throat: no drugs.

Wallace calls this live contraction of attention "abiding." Considering the prospect of refusing his pain medication, it occurs to Gately that "he could do the dextral pain the same way: Abiding. No one single instant of it was unendurable. Here was a second right here: he endured it. What was undealable-with was the thought of all the instants all lined up and stretching ahead, glittering" (IJ 860). The first time he'd really done it, "this inter-beat Present, this sense of endless Now—it had vanished in Revere Holding along with the heaves and chills. He'd returned to himself, moved to sit on the bunk's edge, and ceased to Abide because he no longer had to" (IJ 860). But like Fogle's experience with Obetrol, something had happened. Gately had accidentally been introduced to what things look like on the far side of crushing boredom. And now "he wonders, sometimes, if that's what Ferocious Francis and the rest want him to walk toward: Abiding again between heartbeats; tries to imagine what kind of impossible leap it would take to live that way all the time, by choice, straight: in the second, the Now, walled and contained between slow heartbeats" (IJ 860).

Taken too far, this kind of focus can itself become another kind of escape. Abiding requires that we climb down out of the head and into the body, but it doesn't require a headless body. "Quiet tales sometimes go around the Boston AA community," Wallace gossips, that imagine this project taken to the extreme. These tales tell about "certain incredibly advanced and hard-line recovering persons who have pared away potential escape after potential escape until finally, as the stories go, they end up sitting in a bare chair, nude, in an unfurnished room, not moving but also not sleeping or meditating or abstracting" (IJ 998). These guys are "too advanced to stomach the thought of the potential emotional escape of doing anything whatsoever, and just end up sitting there completely motion- and escape-less until a long time later all that's found in the empty chair is a very fine dusting of off-white ashy stuff that you can wipe away completely with like one damp paper towel" (IJ 998). This urban legend is a parody of abiding that duplicates the original problem on a different level. It takes a fear of the head's intractable flittering so far that it ends up darkly mirroring the very escapism it was meant to counter. This brand of bastardized abiding ends up being an escape from emotional escaping. That's no good either.

Gately is in an especially tough spot, but more ordinary examples are just as germane: reading a tax return, listening to a colleague, driving a car, playing tennis, making dinner. The more ordinary, the better. It's the ordinary itself that abiding will bring back into focus. The aim with abiding is to "occur." Appraising his performance in a match, one of Hal's coaches tells him: "You just never quite occurred out there, kid" (IJ 686). Most of the time, time passes but we fail to occur. We're like Fogle who "wasn't even really aware of what was going on, most of the time" (PK 185). We have an absentee vibe and "give off a slight hum even when at rest" because we can't be where we are (PK 174). To counteract this tendency, the tennis academy students get this advice from their German, broken-English speaking coach: "Move. Travel lightly. Occur. Be *here*. Not in bed or shower or over baconschteam, in the mind. Be *here* in total. Is nothing else. Learn. Try. Drink your green juice" (IJ 461). This is the gospel of abiding: move, try, occur, drink your green juice.

# 27

# Bodies

Returning to the present, you return to the body. Learning how to live in the space between heartbeats depends on rediscovering you have a heart that beats. It means feeling your lungs contract and expand. To find not just your breath but the space between breaths, you'll have "to reach down into parts of yourself you didn't know were there and get down in there and live inside these parts. And the only way to get to them: sacrifice. Suffer. Deny. What are you willing to give" (IJ 119). This is a "religion of the physical" (IJ 169).

As Hal Incandenza's grandfather told his father, "the trick will be transcending that overlarge head, son. Learning to move just the way you already sit still. Living in your body" (IJ 158). Take up a sport. Make your body sweat. Feel it move. Transcend that overlarge head. Take things you know in your head and code them into your flesh. "It's repetition. First last always. It's hearing the same motivational stuff over and over till sheer repetitive weight makes it sink down into the gut" (IJ 117). Let the repetition free your attention. "It's repetitive movements and motions for their own sake, over and over until the accretive weight of the reps sinks the movements themselves down under your like consciousness into the more nether regions, through repetition they sink and soak into the hardware, the C.P.S. The machine-language. The autonomical part that makes you breathe and sweat" (IJ 117). To live in the inter-heartbeat span of the present, you'll have to learn something about the user-unfriendly machine-language of the real. You'll have to be able to read a body's complex tax form. Your head has to be still long enough to remember that it, too, is body. When you get that far, then "the mechanics are wired in. Hardwired in. This frees the head in the remarkablest ways. Just wait" (IJ 118). The head gets freed, not from the body but from its debilitating attempt to do without the body. It gets freed for the body. Or, better, it gets freed *as* body.

Listen, Hal's grandfather says. "Son, you're ten, and this is hard news for somebody ten, even if you're almost five-eleven, a possible pituitary freak. Son, you're a body, son" (IJ 159). You're a body. And the head, though special, can't just go its own way. "That quick little scientific-prodigy's mind she's so proud of and won't quit twittering about: son, it's just neural spasms, those thoughts in your mind are just the sound of your head revving, and head is still just body, Jim. Commit this to memory. Head is body. Jim, brace yourself against my shoulders here for this hard news, at ten: you're a machine a body an object, Jim" (IJ 159). Don't read this as a kind of reductionist screed. It's the head that's always trying to reduce everything to part of itself. Saying that "head is body" doesn't deprive the head of anything but its fantasies. Committing this to memory—head is body, head is body—means affirming that the head, like the body, is real. Though, as a consequence, it also means affirming that the head's reality entails its being opaque, taxing, resistant, and user-unfriendly like every other real thing.

It's not so different from driving a car: "It's an object, Jim, a body, but don't let it fool you, sitting here, mute. It will *respond*. If given its due. With artful care" (IJ 159). But you can't treat bodies disdainfully, impatiently. You have to feel your way down into the machine-language of sensation, like a driver who discovers that the car's body is his own, "who *feels* the big steel body he's inside, who quietly and unnoticed feels the nubbly plastic of the grip of the shift up next to the wheel when he shifts just as he feels the skin and flesh, the muscle and sinew and bone wrapped in gray spiderwebs of nerves in the blood-fed hand" (IJ 159). This won't always be pleasant, but it will be real. And alive. It will feel a bit like coming home. Waking up to find himself in his body, Fogle says: "It wasn't all fun and games. But it did feel *alive*, and that's probably why I liked it. It felt like I actually *owned* myself. Instead of renting or whatever—I don't know" (PK 186).

Meredith Rand finds this same thing happening while she's talking to Drinion. Drinion's attention turned her body on.

During the tête-à-tête with Drinion she'd felt sensuously aroused in a way that had little to do with being excited or nervous, that she'd felt the surface of the chair against her bottom and back and the backs of her legs, and the material of her skirt, and the sides of her shoes against the sides of her feet in hose whose microtextured weave she could also feel, and the feel of her tongue against her teeth's rear and palate, the vent's air against her hairline and the room's other air against her face and arms and the taste of cigarette smoke's residue. At one or two points she'd even felt she could feel the exact shape of her eyeballs against her lids' insides when she blinked—she was aware when she blinked. (PK 494)

Rand, tuned-in, abiding, aware, gets resurrected. Her head gets planted back in her body. She becomes a prophetess, a data mystic, a fact psychic.

There is a kind of grace that shows itself in the body when the body once again has a head. An effortlessness arises. As you "learn to do nothing, with your whole head and body," then "everything will be done by what's around you" (IJ 158). This is the advice that Lyle, the tennis academy guru, gives again and again. "Do not underestimate objects! Lyle says he finds it impossible to overstress this: do *not* underestimate objects" (IJ 394). The head always wants to use its maps instead of the objects themselves. But this is no good. "Do not leave objects out of account. The world, after all, which is radically old, is made up mostly of objects" (IJ 395). When you stop running from bodies, you draw life and strength from them. Don't leave bodies out of account. The world, which is radically old, is nothing but bodies.

# 28

# Prayer

This is very local work. The point of abiding is to loosen the head's grip on its global maps and wake you up to your local neighborhood. The dream of an uppercase Substance gives way to a profusion of lowercase bodies. It makes sense, then, to hear Gately say that, in trying to build a wall around each day, he "feels like he has no access to the Big spiritual Picture" (IJ 443). Feeling like you have no access to the Big Picture might very well mean the practice is working.

Wallace revisits this point repeatedly in *Infinite Jest*. The head has been intertwined so thoroughly with so much of the problem for so long—both feeding it and feeding off it—it's a relief to discover that, at this point, it doesn't really matter what your head thinks. It just matters what your body *does*. Gately's rehab sponsors advise him to start praying, but they couldn't care less if he believes in God. It's irrelevant. Speaking at an AA meeting, Gately says he

> feels about the ritualistic *Please* and *Thank You* prayers rather like a hitter that's on a hitting streak and doesn't change his jock or socks or pre-game routine for as long as he's on the streak. W/sobriety being the hitting streak and whatnot, he explains. The whole church basement is literally blue with smoke. Gately says he feels like this is a pretty limp and lame understanding of a Higher Power: a cheese-easement or unwashed athletic supporter. He says but when he tries to go beyond the very basic rote automatic get-me-through-this-day-please stuff, when he kneels at other times and prays or meditates or tries to achieve a Big-Picture spiritual

understanding of a God as he can understand Him, he feels Nothing—not nothing but *Nothing*, an edgeless blankness that somehow feels worse than the sort of unconsidered atheism he Came In with. (IJ 443)

That edgeless blankness may eventually have some importance of its own when it comes to God, but for now the crucial thing is just to do it. Get on your knees.

Gately asks his sponsors, "How can you pray to a 'God' you believe only morons believe in, still?" Or, how can "you keep getting ritually down on your big knees every morning and night asking for help from a sky that still seems a burnished shield against all who would ask aid of it" (IJ 350)? And the older guys, guys with lots of time under their belts and lots of practice at not paying attention to how much time they have under their belts, say: "It doesn't yet matter what you believe or don't believe. Just Do It they say, and like a shock-trained organism without any kind of independent human will you do exactly like you're told, you keep coming and coming" (IJ 350).

Explanation and understanding are useful at one level and for some things. But not for everything and not all the time. And this is especially true when you think you can get away with substituting an explanation for a solution. If you're speaking in an AA meeting, Wallace says, never be ironic and never attribute responsibility for your condition to any outside causes. "Causal-attribution, like irony, is death" (IJ 370). Causes are real but they're also easy escape routes. "Here there is no Cause or Excuse. It is simply what happened" (IJ 378). Anything that gets in the way of taking local, personal responsibility has to be set aside. "It's not like Boston AA recoils from the idea of responsibility, though. Cause: no; responsibility: yes. It seems like it all depends on which way the arrow of presumed responsibility points" (IJ 376). Does the arrow point down and into the body? Or does it point out and away through the head?

Meredith Rand makes this same point about her time in an institution. Her doctors were in love with explanations. And, worse, they made the mistake of thinking that explanations were treatment. "All that matters is that I was doing it and to stop doing it. That was it. Unlike the doctors and small groups that were all about your feelings and why, as though if you knew why you did it you'd magically be able to stop" (PK 486). This, Rand's future husband tells her, is "the big lie they all bought that made doctors and standard therapy such a waste of time for people like us—they thought that diagnosis was the same as cure. That if you knew why, it would stop. Which is bullshit" (PK 486). It doesn't work like that. "You only stop if you stop" (PK 486).

Prayer follows this same pattern. Prayer won't hand you a Big Picture explanation. It's no good for that. Prayer is a way of practicing responsibility. It's a way of being responsive to what's happening right now, whether that thing is your will or not, whether you are inclined to be grateful for it or not. Prayer is a name for the practice of abiding. Prayer ends up being more like baking a cake than like having a meaningful conversation with your long lost father. Cake boxes come with a cake mix already inside, premixed, and "with directions on the side any eight-year old could read" (IJ 467). There's no need to reinvent the wheel and make the whole thing all metaphysical. "All Gately had to do was for fuck's sake give himself a break and relax and for once shut up and just follow the directions on the side of the fucking box. It didn't matter one fuckola whether Gately like *believed* a cake would result, or whether he *understood* the like fucking baking-chemistry of *how* a cake would result" (IJ 467). Follow the directions, add the ingredients, put it in the oven with your own hands, take everything one local step at a time, and you'll get a cake.

You should consider "that God might regard the issue of whether you believe there's a God or not as fairly low on his/her/its list of things he/she/it's interested in re you" (IJ 205). Though it's also true that, eventually, you may have to reckon with the fact that prayer worked. Or also with the fact that some people *do* believe. Or even with the fact that "certain sincerely devout and spiritually advanced people believe that the God of their understanding helps them find parking places and gives them advice on Mass. Lottery numbers" (IJ 204). Or maybe not. Either way, there's real force to the kind of question that Mario asks Hal one night as they're lying in bed. Mario had watched Hal's match that day. Hal had destroyed his opponent. Everything came easy. He was in his body. His head was clear. The objects around him did a lot of the work for him. Mario says: "I was going to ask if you felt like you believed in God, today, out there, when you were so on" (IJ 40). Hal is tired. And he's tired, in particular, of this question. He bristles at Mario's God-talk: "So tonight to shush you how about if I say I have administrative bones to pick with God, Boo. I'll say God seems to have a kind of laid-back management style I'm not crazy about. I'm pretty much anti-death. God looks by all accounts to be pro-death. I'm not seeing how we can get together on this issue, he and I" (IJ 40). There's real force to the objection Hal lodges against God, but it's blunted by his evasion. Hal's explanation, though smart, is a dodge. Mario didn't ask if, Big Picture style, Hal believed in God. He asked if Hal *felt* like he believed in God when he was playing earlier that day. The difference is crucial. Mario responds: "I don't get how you couldn't feel like you believed, today, out there. It was so *right there*. You moved like you totally believed" (IJ 41). Mario's not asking about what Hal thinks. He's not asking about what Hal's head makes of anything. He's asking about what Hal did. And regardless of what his head says, Hal *did* make a cake.

# 29

# Clichés

Gately is a convert. Whatever his shortcomings, he's come to trust the sturdy clichés that order his recovery. He didn't always feel this way. Like most beginners, he balked at the flood of clichés he was asked to live by. These clichés exhibit none of the sparkle, complexity, or appeal of big, high-powered ideas. As distractions or entertainment, they fail entirely. More, their value depends on this failure. Clichés remind us of things that are ordinary, local, boring, and taxing. They don't rely overmuch on the head.

The strength of a cliché is proportional to its failure to impress. Its power is manifest on the flipside of boredom. "How do trite things get to be trite? Why is the truth usually not just un- but anti-interesting? Because every one of the seminal little mini-epiphanies you have early in AA is always polyesterishly banal" (IJ 358). It's one thing to parrot these platitudes, it's something else to live them. "The clichéd directives are a lot more deep and hard to actually *do*. To try and live by instead of just say" (IJ 273). Some halfway house residents complain to Gately about this, looking for a pass, for some other, more exciting way through their trouble. Incredulous, Randy Lenz asks Gately: "So then at forty-six years of age I came here to learn to live by clichés …. To turn my will and life over to the care of clichés. One day at a time. Easy does it. First things first. Courage is fear that has said its prayers. Ask for help. Thy will not mine be done. It works if you work it. Grow or go. Keep coming back" (IJ 270). Yes. You're to turn your head over to the care of clichés. If you turn over your will—and pray, and keep coming, and don't close your eyes when they start to burn, and don't leave when the audience has gone, and do the next tax return even though there's only five minutes left until quitting time—then something else can happen. An inversion can take place. Your idol can fail. As Gately has it, you may start to make

> this grudging move toward maybe acknowledging that this unromantic, unhip, clichéd AA thing—so unlikely and unpromising, so much the inverse of what they'd come too much to love—might really be able to keep the lover's toothy maw at bay. The process is the neat reverse of what brought you down and In here: Substances start out being so magically great, so much the interior jigsaw's missing piece, that at the start you just know, deep in your gut, that they'll never let you down; you just know it. But they do. And then this goofy slapdash anarchic system of low-rent gatherings and corny slogans and saccharin grins and hideous coffee is so lame you just *know* there's no way it could ever possibly work except for the utterest morons ... and then Gately seems to find out AA turns out to be the very loyal friend he thought he'd had and then lost, when you Came In. (IJ 350, ellipsis original)

The cliché doesn't even pretend to be the uppercase Substance the head wants to see. It offers no magic relief. It promises no other worlds. But "newcomers who abandon common sense and resolve to Hang In and keep coming and then find their cages all of a sudden open, mysteriously after a while, share this sense of deep shock" (IJ 350). They share this deep shock at the power of the cliché, at the strength of the ordinary, at the beauty of the boring, and this shock works like a defibrillator that, with a painful jerk, brings them back from the undead.

This is why rehab needs to be "maximally unironic" (IJ 369). Irony is too ready a defense. It puts too much distance between the head and the body. It tries to invest the ordinary with some superimposed meaning. Instead of building a wall around this moment, irony builds a wall *between* itself and the moment. This defensive wall was supposed to save the head from the world but, instead, it traps it, leaving the head to stew in its own juices. Irony, as a way of life, is pseudo-rebellion. It's all bluster and posture. It leaves untouched the world it refuses. Real rebellion looks like the rigorous practice of

## CLICHÉS

clichés. It looks like turning off the TV. Real rebellion will depend on people who

dare somehow to back away from ironic watching, who have the childish gall actually to endorse and instantiate single-entendre principles. Who treat plain old untrendy human troubles and emotions in U.S. life with reverence and conviction. Who eschew self-consciousness and hip fatigue. These anti-rebels would be outdated, of course, before they even started. Dead on the page. Too sincere. Clearly repressed. Backward, quaint, naïve, anachronistic. Maybe that'll be the point. (SF 81)

Such cliché-practicing, single-entendre, boredom-proof, anachronistic anti-rebels aren't likely to make the news.

# 30

# Epiphany

As near as we can tell, Wallace never settled on a plot for *The Pale King*. One idea he proposed as a possible key to the book's structure was to have the whole thing gear around something really important that never happens. "Something big *threatens* to happen but doesn't actually happen" (PK 544). In this sense, even unfinished, the book succeeds. *The Pale King* is a book that threatens to happen but never quite does; it's never rescued from the troubles of life by the arrival of an uppercase Plot. If Wallace succeeds and gives that world a plot, he risks missing the very world he's trying to write about. If he succeeds and makes his treatment of boredom riveting reading, he risks undermining the point he wants to make about boredom. A cliché that looks important is no longer a cliché.

But—still—something important does happen. Passing through the eye of boredom doesn't leave the world untouched. It doesn't leave us empty-handed. Something occurs. Chris Fogle gets a feel for this when, practicing boredom, he sees something that, before, was obscure. Abiding, he comes to see, he says "that there were depths to me that were not bullshit or childish but profound, and were not abstract but actually much realer than my clothes or self-image, and that blazed in an almost sacred way" (PK 187). More, he discovers how the "most profound parts of me involved not drives or appetites but simple attention, awareness" (PK 187).

But this moment of revelation, the data mystic's epiphany, isn't likely to come when you expect it or in connection with something exciting. In scenarios like that, appetites will likely crowd out awareness. The revelation is more likely to come when you're doing an ordinary thing, in an ordinary way. It's more likely to come in a moment of repose when, sitting still, you're doing the kind of thing all human beings do. In the Enfield Tennis Academy boy's locker room, Hal Incandenza sees Ted Schacht's purple shower thongs poking out from under a stall door and he recognizes the moment. He notes that there's something very human, something very quiet,

> something humble, placid even, about inert feet under stall doors. The defecatory posture is an accepting posture, it occurs to him. Head down, elbows on knees, the fingers laced together between the knees. Some hunched timeless millennial type of waiting, almost religious. Luther's shoes on the floor beneath the chamber pot, placid, possibly made of wood, Luther's 16th-century shoes, awaiting epiphany. The mute quiescent suffering of generations of salesmen in the stalls of train-station johns, heads down, fingers laced, shined shoes inert, awaiting the acid gush. Women's slippers, centurion's dusty sandals, dock-worker's hobnailed boots, Pope's slippers. All waiting, pointing straight ahead, slightly tapping. Huge shaggy-browed men in skins hunched just past the firelight's circle with wadded leaves in one hand, waiting. (IJ 103)

# Afterword

In their widely praised and *New York Times* bestselling book, *All Things Shining: Reading the Western Classics to Find Meaning in a Secular Age*, Hubert Dreyfus and Sean Dorrance Kelly dedicate more than forty pages to reading Wallace and their verdict is severe. On their telling, Wallace is a nihilist. He's an avatar of a willful and godless brand of hyper-individualism. "In Wallace's Nietzschean view," they claim, "we are the sole agents in the universe, responsible for generating out of nothing whatever notion of the sacred and divine there can ever be" (AS 57). For them, Wallace's gospel is a postmodern nightmare. His vision of the sacred is "deeply impoverished" and "there is no sense whatsoever in Wallace that the 'sacred' moments of existence are gifts, so there is no place for gratitude" (AS 48). In short, "there is no joy in Wallace's world" (AS 46). In *All Things Shining*, Wallace is reduced to a foil for Dreyfus and Kelly's own version of postsecular salvation and, as a result, their reading often verges on cartoonish. In general, their take on Wallace is both unconvincing and, it seems to me, uncharitable.

Apart from rhetorical posturing, Dreyfus and Kelly fail to understand Wallace because they don't understand his take on worship. They assume Wallace shares their project. They assume he wants to reinvest our disappointing, disenchanted, secular world with meaning. They mistake Wallace's insistence on the importance of attention for a blind, last-ditch attempt to supercharge some idol with the power to satisfy. They read the moment of disappointment that follows the failure of these idols as evidence that Wallace's own project has failed and, as a result, they miss altogether his most fundamental claim: that these failures are not only inevitable but *critical* to the good news his novels and essays are trying to articulate. They don't see that, for Wallace, the moment of disappointment is the moment of revelation. Given their own position, this isn't surprising. For Dreyfus and Kelly, finding meaning in our secular age depends on generating a transcendent "whoosh!" (their word) and so they can't bring into focus Wallace's attempt to claim the disenchanted "fshzzzt" (my word) of immanence as an epiphany all its own.

Dreyfus and Kelly's case rests on two things: a reading that treats Wallace's medical condition and eventual suicide as a data point that trumps his own texts ("There is no doubt that there are neurophysiological and neurochemical aspects to severe depression, and it seems natural to conclude that Wallace finally succumbed in the face of biological odds. And yet ...") and a pretty elementary phenomenological confusion about the difference between paying attention and willfully imposing meaning (AS 22–23). Let's leave aside their invocations of Wallace's suicide and press, instead, the phenomenological point.

Their smoking gun with respect to Wallace's nihilism is his 2005 commencement address at Kenyon College, eventually published as *This Is Water*. Here, Wallace claims that even the ordinary frictions of daily life can spark a holy conflagration—if we pay attention. The damning passage reads like this:

> If you're automatically sure that you know what reality is and who and what is really important—if you want to operate on your default setting—then you, like me, probably will not consider possibilities that aren't pointless and annoying. But if you've learned how to think, how to pay attention, then you will know you have other options. It will actually be within your power to experience a crowded, hot, slow, consumer-hell-type situation as not only meaningful, but sacred, on fire with the same force that lit the stars—compassion, love, the subsurface unity of all things. (TW 91–93, cf. AS 40)

According to Dreyfus and Kelly, this passage means that, for Wallace, the sacred arises when I, the rugged individual, am able to willfully and imaginatively impose on the bare, nihilistic facts of the world a new, special, redemptive meaning. For them, this passage is paradigmatic of how, in Wallace's world, meaning is "something *we impose* upon experience; there is nothing *given* about it at all" (AS

47, emphasis original). Admittedly, they're quick to lionize Wallace for his courageous efforts in the face of absurdity, but they see right away (and rightly) that this can't possibly work. Meaning can't be wished into existence. These idols will disappoint and Wallace will fail. For them, Wallace is a cautionary tale and the lesson to be learned is sweeping: his failure is symptomatic, "an indication of our metaphysical makeup, of the way our age fails to allow us to tell a coherent story about the meaning of our lives" (AS 25). We should admire our tragic hero. But we should be even more careful to avoid making the same mistakes.

The only problem with this reading is that it runs against the grain of both the passage in question and Wallace's bigger project. In this very passage, Wallace maintains that paying attention requires the *suspension* of your automatic assumption that your maps will fit the world. To pay attention, you have to stop operating "on your default setting" (TW 91). Paying attention is not the work of more and more successfully imposing the maps in your head on a mute world. Paying attention is the work of more and more successfully laying those maps aside in favor of the ground at your feet. The polarity has to get reversed. Paying attention doesn't involve a kind of laser-like intentionality; rather, it involves surrendering to a tractor-beam of counter-intentionality. Phenomenologically, it's not the saturation of a given intuition with my intentions, it's the swamping of my capacity for intentions with a saturating intuition. As Wallace puts it earlier in this same address: "It is extremely difficult to stay alert and attentive instead of getting hypnotized by the constant monologue inside your own head" (TW 50). Clearly, the head's ambitious monologue isn't the good guy in this story.

Wallace is up front about this. I'm not offering a secret, clever, deconstructive reading of his text. "I submit that this is what the real, no-shit value of your liberal arts education is supposed to be about: How to keep from going through your comfortable, prosperous, respectable adult life dead, unconscious, a slave to your head and to your natural default setting of being uniquely, completely, imperially alone day in and day out" (TW 60). Wallace doesn't want to be an Übermensch, weaving new worlds out of nothing. He wants to wake up enough to see that he's not alone and that there's more to the world than his maps. He recognizes that attention, as the grip of a counter-intentionality, is not the invention of meaning so much as its suspension. He knows that this kind of waking up involves the surrender, not the victory, of your individual head.

Dreyfus and Kelly try to buttress their reading of his commencement speech with fragments from *The Pale King*. One section they highlight is a key passage (analyzed above in Chapter 16) about Lane Dean, Jr. struggling with the daily grind of checking tax returns:

> [Lane] did two more returns, then another one, then flexed his buttocks and held to a count of ten and imagined a warm pretty beach with mellow surf as instructed in orientation the previous month. Then he did two more returns, checked the clock real quick, then two more, then bore down and did three in a row, then flexed and visualized and bore way down and did four without looking up once.... After just an hour the beach was a winter beach, cold and gray and the dead kelp like the hair of the drowned, and it stayed that way despite all attempts. (PK 376, cf. AS 32)

Dreyfus and Kelly see Lane Dean, Jr. as a clear example of how Wallace's approach fails. They think that Wallace is *recommending* Dean's attempts to imaginatively conjure meaning as a cure for what ails us. They point out that no matter how hard Lane tries to visualize something beautiful and inviting, no matter how hard he tries to impose meaning, the counterweight of boredom breaks his best efforts. But Dreyfus and Kelly appear oblivious to the fact that, while their analysis of Dean's failure has merit, it is merit borrowed from Wallace himself. They steal Wallace's own critique of Dean and then claim to have discovered it as a critique of Wallace's project.

But they're wrong. Wallace is not interested in defending our hunger for distraction. He's interested in how crushing boredom can set our maps on fire and leave us exposed to the world. Boredom signals the world's resistance to our intentions. It signals a tide of counter-intentionality that can save us from ourselves. Boredom marks the limit of what interests us and by passing through its ascesis—by staying with a person or thing past the limit of our self-interest—life can open onto compassion and fellowship.

As Don Gately emphasizes in *Infinite Jest* (again in a passage that Dreyfus and Kelly puzzlingly cite in support of their own reading), the head is the problem not the solution. "What's unendurable is what his own head could make of it all. What his head could report to him, looking over and ahead and reporting. But he could choose not to listen" (IJ 860). This is the key. "He hadn't quite gotten this before now, how it wasn't just the matter of riding out the cravings for a Substance: everything unendurable was in the head, was the head not Abiding in the Present but hopping the wall and doing a recon and returning with unendurable news you then somehow believed" (IJ 861, cf. AS 36). Abiding is decidedly not the practice of heroically investing the void with meaning. It's the practice of staying open to an embodied present long enough for the world to intervene. Neither the present nor the body are unendurable. It's believing the head that's unendurable. It's investing your maps with the power to save you (or damn you) that ruins you.

Dreyfus and Kelly are clear enough about Wallace's project to recognize that, on some level, their critique doesn't fit. But rather than reconsidering their critique, they take these instances as evidence of an unresolved contradiction in Wallace's work. In the book's concluding chapter, they discuss Wallace's well-known essay about Roger Federer's beauty and grace on the tennis court and admit that Wallace is on to something. Federer's tennis—like many examples explored at even greater length in *Infinite Jest*—embodies for Wallace what it means to abide. His athleticism displays what it means to be present and occur. "The human beauty we're talking about here is beauty of a particular type; it might be called kinetic beauty. Its power and appeal are universal. It has nothing to do with sex or cultural norms. What it seems to have to do with, really, is human beings' reconciliation with the fact of having a body" (BF 8). Keen to draw on sports examples themselves, Dreyfus and Kelly have to acknowledge that

> David Foster Wallace, more than most, had a strong sense for sacred moments like this. Perhaps such a claim will sound surprising: after all, the main point of our chapter on Wallace was to highlight the nihilistic strain in his thought. But although a kind of willful Nietzschean nihilism dominates Wallace's work, he was an amazingly receptive writer. Indeed, he seems to have resonated with most of the varied and incompatible phenomena

that animate our contemporary world. In particular, one finds a strong counterstrain to Wallace's nihilism in his writings on the sacred moments of sport. (AS 194)

But these aren't counterstrains. They're Wallace's own gospel. Wallace *is* an amazingly receptive writer. He did have a strong sense for sacred moments like this. And he did resonate, sometimes painfully, with the most varied and incompatible phenomena that animate our contemporary world. But he didn't manage this despite being a nihilist. He managed it because he wasn't one.

# Permissions

Selections from the following materials are used by permission of the David Foster Wallace Literary Trust:

David Foster Wallace, *Both Flesh and Not: Essays* (New York: Little, Brown and Company, 2012).

David Foster Wallace, *Consider the Lobster and Other Essays* (New York: Little Brown and Company, 2005).

David Foster Wallace, *Infinite Jest* (New York: Little, Brown and Company, 1996).

David Foster Wallace, *The Pale King* (New York: Little, Brown and Company, 2011).

David Foster Wallace, *A Supposedly Fun Thing I'll Never Do Again: Essays and Arguments* (New York: Little, Brown and Company, 1997).

David Foster Wallace, *This Is Water: Some Thoughts, Delivered on a Significant Occasion, about Living a Compassionate Life* (New York: Little, Brown and Company, 2009).

# Bibliography

Burn, Stephen J., ed. *Conversations with David Foster Wallace*. Jackson: University Press of Mississippi, 2012.

Dostoevsky, Fyodor. *Notes from Underground.* Translated and edited by Michael R. Katz. New York: W. W. Norton and Company, 2001.

Dreyfus, Hubert and Sean Dorrance Kelly. *All Things Shining: Reading the Western Classics to Find Meaning in a Secular Age*. New York: Free Press, 2011.

Franzen, Jonathan. *Farther Away*. New York: Farrar, Straus and Giroux, 2013.

Lipsky, David. *Although of Course You End Up Becoming Yourself: A Road Trip with David Foster Wallace*. New York: Broadway Books, 2010.

Wallace, David Foster. *Both Flesh and Not: Essays*. New York: Little, Brown and Company, 2012.

Wallace, David Foster. *Consider the Lobster and Other Essays*. New York: Little, Brown and Company, 2005.

Wallace, David Foster. *Infinite Jest*. New York: Little, Brown and Company, 1996.

Wallace, David Foster. *The Pale King*. New York: Little, Brown and Company, 2011.

Wallace, David Foster. *A Supposedly Fun Thing I'll Never Do Again: Essays and Arguments*. New York: Little, Brown and Company, 1997.

Wallace, David Foster. *This Is Water: Some Thoughts, Delivered on a Significant Occasion, about Living a Compassionate Life*. New York: Little, Brown and Company, 2009.

# Index

abiding 91–4
addiction 17–19, 26, 36–7, 91–3
analysis–paralysis 18, 37
atheism xi, 101–2
attention 6, 69–72, 81–2, 92–3, 107, 110–11
awareness 81–2, 107

beauty 47–9
belief 99–102
boredom 30, 77–80, 87, 112

castration 25
clichés 103–5, 107
commercials 44–5
contortions 15–16
counter-intentionality 70, 111–12

data mystics 87–9, 107
death 57–8, 64, 74
despair 25–8, 59
disappointment xi, 25–8
distraction 7, 29–30, 36, 65–7, 78, 112
Dostoevsky 2
Dreyfus, Hubert 109–14

embodiment 95–7, 113
Eschaton 10

focus 6, 69–72, 81–2, 92–3
Franzen, Jonathan 1

God 101–2

hell 45
heroism 84–5

idols x, xii, 22, 62, 109–11
immanence xii

indifference 73–5
irony 39–41, 84, 100, 104–5

Kelly, Sean Dorrance 109–14

levitation 29, 69–70
Lipsky, David 2–3
luxury cruise 26–7, 59–62

maps 9–12
masks 43–6

nihilism 73, 75, 84, 109–14

Obetrol 81–2

pamper 27–8
prayer 57, 99–102

religion xi, xiii
revelation xii–xiii, 80, 87–9, 107

shit 52–3, 61–2, 108
silence 65–6
substance abuse 17–18, 37, 51, 91–3
success 23–4
suicide 1

taxes 13–14, 56–7, 65
television x, 6, 31–4, 36, 39–40, 79–80
time 51–3, 55–7, 63–4, 78
transcendence x, 32, 67, 77

video telephony 43–4

worship xii, 22, 109–10

www.ingramcontent.com/pod-product-compliance
Lightning Source LLC
Chambersburg PA
CBHW050140240426
43673CB00043B/1747